10.5.77

BRAZIL
IN THE
SEVENTIES

BRAZIL IN THE SEVENTIES

RIORDAN ROETT, EDITOR

American Enterprise Institute for Public Policy Research
Washington, D.C.

Riordan Roett is director of Latin American studies at The Johns Hopkins School of Advanced International Studies in Washington, D.C.

Library of Congress Cataloging in Publication Data

Main entry under title:

Brazil in the seventies.

(Foreign policy ; 1) (AEI studies ; 132)
    1. Brazil—Economic conditions—1945-   —Addresses, essays, lectures. 2. Brazil—Foreign economic relations—Addresses, essays, lectures. 3. Brazil—Foreign relations—1930-   —Addresses, essays, lectures. I. Roett, Riordan, 1938-
II. Series. III. Series: American Enterprise Institute for Public Policy Research. AEI studies ; 132.
HC187.B868   330.9'81'06   76-54880
ISBN 0-8447-3230-3

Printed in the United States of America

CONTENTS

1985317

INTRODUCTION

Riordan Roett

Brazil both impresses and shocks those interested in Latin America specifically and the Third World in general. Since the military overthrow of the government of João Goulart in 1964, a coalition of military officers and civilian technocrats has changed the once prevalent image of Brazil as a "sleeping giant" or an exotic tropical Eden. Economic growth rates unmatched in the Third World have prompted an important debate on income distribution and social equity. Brazil's present authoritarian political system has led to heated discussions over the future of representative, participatory politics in Brazil. Violations of human rights by military and civilian security units and growing awareness of international criticism of such violations remain a source of serious internal division. The plight of the Brazilian Northeast—an internationally recognized region of shocking underdevelopment—coexists with the urban sophistication of cities such as Rio de Janeiro and São Paulo.

The essays published here address aspects of these contradictions in contemporary Brazilian society. The Brazil Seminar Series under whose auspices these essays were originally presented was sponsored by the Washington Center of Foreign Policy Research and the Latin American Studies Program of the Johns Hopkins University School of Advanced International Studies, with the support of the American Enterprise Institute. In a series of four meetings in March 1976 the papers were discussed by a small audience of government officials, Brazilian and North American scholars, and representatives of international organizations. The primary focus of the papers is the international aspects of Brazilian development. Professor Werner Baer's paper carefully examines the post-1964 economic expansion or "miracle" in an effort to deal with the extent to which economic

1

growth supported socioeconomic development in Brazilian secrecy. Baer also focuses on the current crisis in the Brazilian economy, which is seen in the context of the worldwide economic *malaise*, and addresses the role played by short-term external phenomena or "internal contradictions" in determining the course of economic performance. The new and growing international economic role of Brazil is addressed in Dr. William R. Cline's paper. In a cogent summary of the development of the foreign economic sector, he concludes that the long-run prospects for Brazilian exports are strong. While serious problems remain—the growing foreign debt, overvalued exchange rates, continuing inflation, and a high level of imports—Brazil has a "trump card" in its natural resources. Employing Hotelling's theory of exhaustible resources, Cline discusses the impressive natural resource potential of Brazil.

Cline's data confirm the growing significance of Brazil within the international economic system. Among non-oil-exporting countries, Brazil ranks first in exports. In total imports, Brazil ranks first among the developing states, surpassing even the oil-rich countries. The role as pragmatic leader that Brazil has begun to exert in international economic meetings and negotiations will probably serve as a model for future action, allowing Brazil to play a broker's role between the North, or industrialized countries, and the South or Third World nations seeking to reorder international economic and political priorities.

No attempt to consider contemporary Brazil would be complete without recognition of the great debate about dependency that has raged since 1964. Professor Robert A. Packenham's paper is a startling and refreshing analysis of dependency theory and its application to Brazil. In five facets of possible national dependence, Packenham finds that Brazil has grown less dependent since 1964 in three —these being the total of national resources and productive capacity, the skill of the national leadership in using resources and productive capacity, and the degree of external influence over the determination of national goals. Brazil is found to be generally but not uniformly less dependent in one facet, that being the nature of external penetration of national resources and productive capacity. And it is generally more dependent in the degree of penetration of national resources and productive capacity by external economic factors.

Brazil's role in the international political system is imaginatively reviewed in Professor Thomas E. Skidmore's paper. Skidmore argues that economics will determine the foreign policy of Brazil for the foreseeable future. The demand for increasing supplies of energy, the

2

emphasis on export-oriented growth, and the need for technology and other imports justify such a determination. Brazil will attempt to diversify its economic linkages both to decrease an historical dependence on the United States and to increase its own international bargaining power.

As Brazil seeks to move toward great-power status, domestic elites will continue to manifest a generally pro-United States bias. Increasingly, Brazil will seek to expand its contacts with the Third World as well as with the industrialized states. Flexible and non-ideological, Brazil's defense of its core foreign policy interests will not be deterred by traditional friendships. While the February 21, 1976, memorandum, signed during Secretary Kissinger's visit to Brasilia, reinforces the old idea that Brazil and the United States have mutual interests, it need not guarantee a relationship without conflict between the two countries in the future.

From these four essays there emerges a profile of Brazil that emphasizes pragmatic moderation in international economic and political affairs on the one hand and a domestic authoritarian political system combined with a disregard for questions of economic redistribution and social justice on the other. On the surface, the two apparently discordant themes present a contradictory and perplexing image of Brazil as it becomes a regional power as well as an influential international actor. To understand the dynamics of contemporary Brazil, it is useful to examine the following issues that appear (implicitly or explicitly) in all the essays. Together they provide a loose framework for speculating about future Brazilian change.

First and foremost, the power of the Brazilian state must be stressed, as well as the role of Brazil in national and international development emphasized. Previously, I have termed such authority as patrimonial, that is,

> the creation and maintenance of a highly flexible and pater-
> nalistic public order, dedicated to its own preservation and
> the preservation of the unity of the nation-state, whether
> under imperial, republican, or military tutelage. The patri-
> monial state in Brazil is first and foremost a bureaucratic
> state in that the authority of public order is maintained by
> the administrative apparatus of the central government.[1]

Since the "Revolution" of March 31, 1964, the authority of the centralized state has increased and indeed has come to dominate the process of change in Brazil. Baer and Cline both provide data that

---

[1] Riordan Roett, *Brazil: Politics in a Patrimonial Society* (Boston: Allyn and Bacon, Inc., 1973), p. 29.

confirm the emergent economic role of the state. The determination of the political elites—both civilian and military—to postpone or perhaps preclude income redistribution and social justice from becoming realizable goals indicates the power these elites exercise in the name of the state.

The post-1964 decision to increase state authority in the economic realm, as the basis for national and international development, explicitly justified the cancellation of the representative political system and the continuation of forms of social control precluding mass participation in the development process. A new constitution, hastily organized political parties, a dramatic increase in the powers of the executive, a further diminution of the influence of the individual states—these and other decisions transferred authority to and consolidated it in the hands of a centralized bureaucratic elite acting on behalf of the state.

A determination to modernize Brazil economically, first through stabilization and then by an export-oriented growth program, accompanied the modernization and reorganization of the political system. The social implications of these economic and political changes are seen in part through the concentration of income and the failure of redistribution. The continuing unwillingness of the state apparatus to move against the social and economic backwardness of the Northeast region is a dramatic illustration of the regime's development orientation.

In 1970 the Northeast accounted for 30.3 percent of the national population, but for only 12.2 percent of national income and only 5.6 percent of national industrial production. The region has been afflicted with devastating (albeit sporadic) droughts since the last century and is comparable to the most underdeveloped areas of the Third World. Various Brazilian regimes have attempted, with little success, to alleviate the misery in the region—indeed, the United States, in a "showcase" Alliance for Progress undertaking, tried to deal with the socioeconomic ills of the Northeast. To date, little has been accomplished: moreover, since 1964, government policy has deliberately emphasized state-determined growth goals at the cost of attacking regional underdevelopment. David Goodman, reviewing the Brazilian economic miracle and its impact on the urban poor in the Northeast, stated:

efficiency criteria also are evident in the design of public expenditure policies and the heavy concentration of investment resources in transportation, power, communications and secondary activities. Capital formation to expand such

4

social services as public health, sanitation, education and housing, which have a more direct impact on the poorer, less privileged groups of the community, has been seriously neglected.[2]

And in examining post-1970 regional policy innovations, he commented that "the equity-related and re-distributive components of these new schemes have atrophied or been abandoned entirely."[3]

The elites, with these goals in mind, have employed economic growth programs to further state power and efficiency at the cost of social equity and redistributive claims. The role of state institutions in all aspects of the economy, and the capacity of the state to use national policy making to avoid social issues is an important aspect of recent Brazilian development. Critics of the regime argue that a point of no return will soon be reached where it will be impossible to ignore social claims; others believe that there is a far greater than recognized capacity within the system for the poor to benefit from the "trickle down" effect of greater economic concentration and growth. In any case, as long as the economic demands of the middle and upper income groups are satisfied, there is little possibility of organized, effective pressure for greater social responsiveness.[4]

The social equity question should be viewed in relation to the political changes introduced since 1964. As Thomas Skidmore suggests in his essay in this volume, the prospects for any short-term alteration of the existing institutional and power structures are limited. (This is the second important theme running through the essays.) The low level of political institutionalization during the pre-1964 period, combined with the weakness of interest group and pluralist political activity historically, helped prepare the way for the imposition of the authoritarian regime now in power. The old political elite either subordinated itself to the new realities or disappeared. The old party system was abolished and two new parties were created (one a government party and the other a way station

---

[2] D. E. Goodman, "The Brazilian Economic 'Miracle' and Regional Policy: Some Evidence from the Urban Northeast," *Journal of Latin American Studies*, vol. 8, no. 1 (May 1976), pp. 6-7.

[3] Ibid., p. 7.

[4] For an overview and summary of the contrasting approaches, see Douglas H. Graham and José Roberto Mendonça de Barros, "The Brazilian Economic Miracle Revisited: Private and Public Sector Initiative in a Market Economy," unpublished manuscript; Werner Baer, "The Brazilian Boom, 1968-72: An Explanation and Interpretation," *World Development*, vol. 1, no. 8 (August 1973); and Albert Fishlow, "Reflections on Post-1964 Economic Policy in Brazil," in Alfred Stepan, ed., *Authoritarian Brazil: Origins, Policies, and Future* (New Haven, Conn.: Yale University Press, 1973).

for those opposed to the regime but unimportant enough to escape regime reprisals). The Congress, opened and closed at executive whim, lost even its former prerogative of influencing policy making. The recent failure of President Geisel's policy of decompression [5] (relaxation of the tight controls exercised over political life) confirmed for many observers the unlikelihood of short-term liberalization. The dramatic (albeit expected) victory of the opposition Brazilian Democratic Movement (MDB) in the congressional elections of 1974 has done little to alter the realities of state control. The possibility of another MDB victory in municipal elections scheduled for late 1976 is not seen by most observers as the occasion for concessions by the government or a new effort at relaxation. The preference of the civilian technocratic elite for a formally democratic political system, although it represents the real interests of a small minority of the population, and the clear military preference for a strong non-participatory regime, indicate the unlikelihood of profound political changes in the near future. The present political system provides minimally representative institutions, within a façade of parliamentary democracy, and guarantees internal security and political stability.

The continuation of the present system will provide the political mechanism by which state economic and social policies are carried out and by which they are justified. To support Brazilian greatness, a concentration of power is required, and opposition is therefore disloyalty. Subversion remains a palpable threat to the stability and therefore the growth and progress of the Brazilian state. Competitive politics is a breeding ground for anti-regime elements and cannot be tolerated. A long-range need for liberalization is admitted by some, but the elite now in power is willing to forgo consideration of such structural modifications for a number of years.

It is important to note that Brazil is not a totalitarian state. It is an authoritarian state, which means that there are undefined but well understood limits on freedom of the press, political debate, access to judicial protection, and other prerequisites to a more open society. Those who refuse to follow the norms established for political expression are dealt with harshly, as the urban guerrillas of the late 1960s and early 1970s discovered.

The authoritarian tradition in Brazil is an old one. Whether one terms this tradition patrimonial, patriarchical, organic-statist, corporationist, or whatever, it is part of the political history of the state. Brazilian authoritarianism is characterized by a willingness to com-

---

[5] Fernando Pedreira, "Decompression in Brazil?" *Foreign Affairs*, vol. 53, no. 3 (April 1975).

promise, to be flexible, to respond pragmatically to new economic needs, and to avoid open and disruptive conflict, save in those instances when the survival of the regime is thought to be challenged. It is a tradition that survives because of its capacity to coopt potential dissidents and to satisfy the economic and status needs of key elite groups.

Brazil's dependence or lack of dependence is a third theme throughout these essays. The power of the state, the generation of new national resources, the productive capacity of the system, and the skill of the elites in combining resources and capacity to confront the international environment work increasingly in Brazil's favor. Rather than an increasingly dependent nation-state, Brazil is an increasingly autonomous actor, both in internal state authority and in the ability of national leaders to determine major developmental goals and values without external referents. The history of state development since 1964, when objectively analyzed, reveals a vast increase in the capacity of the state to avoid an external veto of its goals and of its capability of neutralizing or controlling potential dissident elements within. While some forms of dependency do exist in Brazil, and will continue to exist, as in all nation-states today, Brazil's record in expanding the possibilities of state-determined growth has grown increasingly clear.

A fourth and final theme to be noted is the emergent international influence of Brazil.[6] The need for an expansion of Brazil's international role has been a recurring motif of the post-1964 regime. Economic growth, social peace, and political stability have all been viewed as necessary antecedents of international influence. Social peace and political stability, imposed by the regime, have allowed a maximum effort for state-determined economic growth policies. Those policies have permitted Brazil to take advantage of new and important structural change in the international economic and political systems.

While the prevailing wisdom is that Brazil's "special relationship" with the United States will continue, it is important to remember that international autonomy (both economic and political) has given Brazil a range of policy options previously unavailable. National interests, as perceived by the regime, have led Brazil to deviate from United States foreign policy in recent years. Both the Cline and Skidmore essays indicate areas in which divergence has occurred— the 200-mile territorial limit, bargaining positions on international

---

[6] I have discussed this theme in greater detail in "Brazil Ascendant: International Relations and Geopolitics in the Late 20th Century," *Journal of International Affairs*, vol. 29, no. 2 (Fall 1975).

economic issues, the vote in the United Nations against Zionism in 1975, and the nuclear agreement with West Germany over vociferous United States opposition. These illustrate the wide range of areas in which Brazilian decision makers have broken with the United States. It may well be that the divergence is of minimal significance politically —that the traditional dependent relationship will survive and flourish as Brazil assumes an increasingly moderate international role. But there is the possibility of a newly independent Brazilian foreign policy, that—while not aimed to conflict with the United States—will respond to state-determined international objectives that disagree with U.S. objectives.

Moreover, there is the possibility that a new generation of military and civilian elites, trained within a new concept of the Brazilian state, will see the country's future in terms different from those of the postwar/Cold War generation that has dominated the state apparatus since 1964. The differences between the United States and Brazil over the nuclear agreement, and the alleged hostility to the United States among some of the younger leaders, may result in a lessening of traditional ties with, and dependence on, the United States. That possibility in no way means that outright conflict is probable or possible; but it is prudent for us to understand the magnitude of the international emergence of Brazil and for United States decision makers to be wary of employing outdated and nostalgic models in setting foreign policy responses to Brazilian actions.

The themes of state authority, basic structural modifications of the political system, a reevaluation of dependence, and a more dynamic international role reflect the noteworthy changes in Brazilian development in the last decade. The internal questions of a social and economic nature, present in 1964, remain highly relevant today. The dynamic tension created by international goals and national constraints will determine Brazil's influence in the remaining decades of this century. The essays in this volume are an effort to elucidate both the problems and the prospects for Brazilian development.

1

BRAZIL'S CHANGING ROLE IN THE INTERNATIONAL SYSTEM: IMPLICATIONS FOR U.S. POLICY

Thomas E. Skidmore

Brazil's Economic Prospects

Resources and the Present Economic Crisis. Brazil has one of the richest natural resource bases of any country in the world. The fourth-largest nation in territory, it enjoys vast reserves of virtually every mineral resource except coal and oil, although off-shore discoveries may ameliorate that deficiency. The availability of a large unskilled labor pool has helped the government to enforce a low wage policy (by repression when deemed necessary) thereby strengthening Brazil's export position by keeping labor costs down.[1] Large tracts of uncultivated or undercultivated land, especially in the West and Center-South regions, have made possible continuous growth in agricultural production with relatively low capital inputs. Thus, between 1968 and 1975 Brazil was able to resume the drive for development (defined as high gross domestic product [GDP] growth rates) achieved in 1949–61.[2] This was a new fulfillment of Brazil's long-predicted potential—the predictions having been so frustratingly frequent that in the de-

An earlier version of this paper was presented to the Survey Discussion Group on International Aspects of Brazil's Development at the Council on Foreign Relations in New York on January 22, 1976. I am grateful to the members of that group for their comments and suggestions and especially to Acting Director of Studies Abraham Lowenthal for his careful critique. Equally helpful comments came from participants in the Brazil Seminar at the School of Advanced International Studies where a later version of the paper was presented on March 15, 1976. I am indebted to Peter De Shazo for research assistance.

[1] The most reliable nongovernmental source on real wages is Departamento Intersindical de Estatística e Estudos Socio-Econômicos [DIEESE], "Dez anos de política salarial" in *Estudos Socioeconômicos*, vol. 1, no. 3 (August 1975).

[2] Much of the extensive literature on Brazil's post-1964 economic record is cited in the chapters by Werner Baer and William Cline in this volume.

spair of the early 1960s Brazilian cynics dismissed their land as "yesterday's country of tomorrow."

But 1976 opened on far less happy economic news.[3] In 1975 growth was down significantly (although still positive in per capita terms) and inflation proved higher than government planners had hoped for. Most disturbing was the large deficit in the balance of payments, partially resulting from an import boom (led by capital goods) fueled by speculative fever at the expectation of impending restrictions that were finally imposed in November. The new government (President Geisel having succeeded President Médici in March 1974) was slow to react to the ballooning current account deficit for several reasons. First, it was feeling its way, and may have avoided painful economic measures because it feared that their unpopularity would endanger its limited attempt at political "decompression." Second, Brazil's unprecedentedly large foreign exchange reserves ($6.4 billion at the end of 1973) offered short-term room for maneuver. Third, the necessary import restrictions (or import pricing policies) were bound to hit hardest at two of the economy's most dynamic sectors: consumer durable goods and public investment. Time ran out in late 1975. President Geisel delivered the somber news and warned of the need to redouble efforts on the export front.

Brazil's greatest assets are its resource base and its established expertise in macroeconomic management. By 1973 Brazilian policy makers had developed a bevy of sophisticated fiscal and monetary instruments. By using them carefully in demand management, and by promoting a highly successful export drive, they had laid a base for further development. During 1973, however, economic policy making, and even official statistics, were significantly distorted in order to hold inflation beneath the target maximum announced by President Médici at the beginning of the year. In short, Finance Minister Delfim Neto, whose seven years of policy dominance continued until March 1974, subordinated economic management to protecting the president's political prestige. More important, policy makers reacted too slowly to ominous trends in foreign financing and the trade balance. In 1974 Brazil's imports doubled (from $6.2 billion to $12.6 billion) while exports showed a healthy but far more modest increase (from $6.2 billion to $7.9 billion). The rapid increase in the trade deficit began during the last months of Delfim Neto's economic stewardship but became clearly established only after Mário

---

[3] Data on Brazil's balance of payments and foreign indebtedness are taken from "Dívida Externa Brasileira: Algumas Considerações," *Conjuntura Econômica*, vol. 30, no. 4 (April 1976).

Henrique Simonsen assumed the Treasury in 1974. The timing was similar for the alarming rise in Brazil's foreign debt, which went from $12.6 billion at the end of 1973 to approximately $22 billion by the end of 1975. The delay in responding suggests costly indecision on the highest levels.

The Importance of Exports. What can we say of the prospects for the Brazilian economy over the next five years? First, how serious is the current crisis? An interruption in the seven-year record of 10 percent annual GDP growth is hardly surprising, especially in view of the worldwide recession that began in the fall of 1974. Brazil's continued positive per capita growth rate and reasonably controlled inflation in 1975 are proof both of its formidable natural advantages and of the benefits of previous economic management. Now once again, as so often in the past, Brazil's growth prospects depend upon the external sector: the first priority is to continue export promotion in order to pay for essential imports and service the foreign debt, which has grown rapidly with the boom.

Brazil's export effort since 1964 has been impressive. Years of preparation were necessary—years of simplifying regulations, facilitating transport, promoting export-mindedness among entrepreneurs, experimenting with a wide range of incentives. The work of these years began to pay off after 1968. With 1966 as a base year, Brazil's export index had jumped to 458 by the end of 1974. Despite the world recession, Brazil managed to increase exports to $8.7 billion in 1975 from $7.9 billion in 1974. To attribute this record almost entirely to more favorable terms of trade is misleading, inasmuch as the greatly altered composition of exports directly reflects government success in facilitating a timely response to trends in the world market.[4] To confirm the point, one need only compare the Brazilian case to that of Argentina, whose export earnings experienced little growth because policy makers and exporters failed to capitalize on the boom in world trade. Given reasonably full employment policies in the developed world (which may well hinge on the policies of the Carter administration, and given continued export aggressiveness by Brazil (accompanied by realistic exchange rate and import pricing policies), the country's export earnings should continue to grow at a healthy rate.

---

[4] Too little credit is given to government policies in Albert Fishlow, "Foreign Trade Regimes and Economic Development: Brazil," a paper presented to the Survey Discussion Group on International Aspects of Brazil's Development, Council on Foreign Relations, April 8, 1975 (reproduced from typescript).

Foreign Inputs: How Severe a Balance-of-Payments Constraint? Three key foreign inputs will remain the focus of government concern, as they have been since 1945: capital, technology, and fuel. To acquire these three in sufficient quantity will force Brazil to continue the effort at diversifying its economic dependence by reducing its primary reliance on the United States. The country will turn increasingly to West Europe and Japan for capital and technology, but oil will prove far more difficult. Brazil has launched a number of attempts to obtain cheaper oil, including direct barter deals with North African producers and the opening of Brazilian oil fields to bids for risk contracts by international oil firms (mostly U.S.). Hopes for future oil supplies from Angola were a factor leading Brazil to be one of the first non-Communist countries to recognize the pro-Soviet faction as the official Angolan government. Brazil will also aggressively seek growing markets in the developing world, as well as in the non-U.S. industrial economies, for its increasingly wide range of primary products and manufactured goods.

Brazil is once again facing the kind of balance-of-payments constraint that has bedevilled the country for most of the post-1945 era. Growth is bound to suffer as a result of the import restrictions, since a large part of imports are essential for investment. The first casualty will be the ambitious goals outlined in the Second National Development Plan (Projecto do II Plano Nacional 1974). Accelerated import-substituting industrialization is needed in, ironically, the most import-intensive area: capital goods. The balance-of-payments problem is further exacerbated by the foreign debt burden that claimed the extraordinarily high level of 41 percent of export earnings in 1975.[5] An intelligent and aggressive foreign trade policy should aid Brazil to weather this crisis, although in the short run a preoccupation with international credit-worthiness may overshadow priorities for domestic economic growth.

How Dynamic a Model? Can the Brazilian growth continue, even given relative success in the external sector? In the late 1960s the underconsumptionist school of critics answered with a resounding "no." The only solution to the impending stagnation, they argued, was income redistribution (direct and indirect) to broaden demand and thereby sustain growth. Whatever one may think of the distributionist consequences of the post-1964 model, lack of demand has *not* been a problem since 1967. Indeed, the most creative of the underconsumptionist critics, such as Celso Furtado and Maria da Con-

---

[5] "Dívida Externa Brasileira," p. 76.

ceição Tavares, have gone on from their early positions to analyze *how* the model has managed to remain dynamic.[6] Given the unreconstructed underconsumptionists' poor record of prediction so far, we are justified in regarding their views skeptically now. The same could be said of the undersaving or underinvestment critiques. Both require us to assume that the Brazilian government will fail to use the readily available and highly powerful policy instruments to stimulate savings or investment, if indicated. The government record of the last seven years should lead us to doubt the probability of such incompetence. Nonetheless, growth will be more difficult than in the past. Even government optimists are predicting only 4 to 5 percent for 1976.

What of the possibility that government responses to the demands for greater social justice (that is, for more distributionist policies) might endanger the growth rate? Scholarly research has shown that a more egalitarian incomes policy than that now in force could be carried out with minimal impact on growth, although in practice measures might prove more disruptive.[7] Nonetheless, one can be skeptical that any significant policy shift toward more equal distribution is likely. Despite the frequent rhetorical commitments by politicians, including the present government, rapid large-scale changes in income distribution directed by capitalist governments have been extremely rare. Why should we expect an authoritarian government, apparently well able to control and manipulate the opposition (more on this later), to alter its development strategy in any serious way? One possible answer: because the government, misguided or not, thinks it ought to or must take such steps.

This seems implausible, in part because the growth model has been managed so as to reward precisely that elite which is responsible for its design and operation. They are the technocratic, managerial, and professional elite whose incomes have improved handsomely since 1968. Engineers and university professors (Federal and São Paulo universities) now take home salaries equivalent to those of

---

[6] Celso Furtado, *Analise do "modelo" brasileiro* (Rio de Janeiro: Ed. Civilização Brasileira, 1972) and *O mito do desenvolvimento econômico* (Rio de Janeiro: Editora Paz e Terra, 1974), and Maria da Conceição Tavares, *Da substituição de importações ao capitalismo financeiro: ensaios sôbre economia brasileira* (Rio de Janeiro: Zahar Editores, 1973).

[7] William R. Cline, *Potential Effects of Income Redistribution on Economic Growth: Latin American Cases* (New York: Praeger Publishers, 1972); Samuel A. Morley and Gordon W. Smith, "The Effect of Changes in the Distribution of Income on Labor, Foreign Investment, and Growth in Brazil," in Alfred Stepan, ed., *Authoritarian Brazil: Origins, Policies, and Future* (New Haven, Conn.: Yale University Press, 1973).

their North American counterparts, while the market has pushed the pay of Brazilian business managers of U.S. multinationals above that of their U.S. supervisors, to the chagrin of home offices. At the same time, the dynamic Center-South has drawn waves of rural migrants many of whom have experienced great individual economic mobility, some reaching the high-paying ranges of the urban "labor aristocracy." None of this alters the fact that enormous inequalities persist, as numerous data (both official and unofficial) make clear.[8]

Relatively minor gestures toward social welfare (which is how I would define the net redistribution effects of such programs as the Programa de Integração Social (PIS) and the small increase in real wages resulting from the minimum wage decisions in 1975) can be made with little impact on overall development strategy. In practice, the much-publicized PIS-type programs will probably turn out to be little more than a new means of generating forced savings to finance public sector investment. Furthermore, over the next year or two the Brazilian government may find itself under less heat on the income distribution question as academic economists raise doubts about the methodological and empirical bases of previous critiques.[9] In sum, over the next five years it seems unlikely that the Brazilian government will choose to sacrifice, or feel itself forced to sacrifice, growth for social welfare, if in fact a large-scale trade-off would result from policies significantly more distributionist than those now practiced.

The Almighty Automobile. There will, however, be problems—perhaps severe—in maintaining the durable goods-oriented consumption boom, *as it has developed since 1968.* The chief symbol and the chief artifact of that boom has been the automobile. In 1975 vehicle production (overwhelmingly concentrated in private passenger cars) exceeded 900,000 units, which compares interestingly with Britain's production of 1,643,000 units last year. Yet the much-coveted symbol has become the focus of almost every problem inherent in the Brazilian economic model. Most obvious in this connection is the oil crisis. With the huge boost in the cost of imported petroleum, on which Brazil depends for 80 percent of its consumption, the annual foreign exchange burden of satisfying upper- middle-income consum-

---

[8] The data are made clear in Ricardo Tolipan and Arthur Carlos Tinelli, eds., *A controvérsia sobre distribuição de renda e desenvolvimento* (Rio de Janeiro: Zahar Editores, 1975), and DIEESE, "Dez anos de política salarial."

[9] Carlos Geraldo Langoni, *Distribuição de renda e desenvolvimento econômico do Brasil* (Rio de Janeiro: Editora Expressão e Cultura, 1973), and Samuel A. Morley and Jeffrey G. Williamson, "Growth, Wage Policy, and Inequality: Brazil during the Sixties," mimeographed (Madison, Wis.: Social Systems Research Institute, University of Wisconsin, Madison, Workshop Series, July 1975).

ers' penchant to own their own vehicle has more than doubled over the last two years (Brazil's oil import bill in 1975 was more than two times the value of *all* imports a decade earlier). This highly expensive fuel consumption—much of it for nonessential convenience and recreation—is competing for foreign exchange needed to buy vital technology and capital goods. The same could be said of the steel imports needed in 1975 to supply the auto industry, whose demands currently exceed Brazil's steel-making capacity.

Beyond this balance-of-payments burden of the private auto boom are the problems of traffic congestion and pollution in the major cities, especially Rio and São Paulo. Despite the Brazilian national government's studied hostility to internationally coordinated environmental concerns (*vide* Brazil's uncooperative stand at Stockholm in 1972), local concern over severe atmospheric pollution and enormous traffic delays is growing. A chief culprit, especially in São Paulo, is the private auto.

Yet a significant drop in the growth rate of auto production, which did occur in 1975, will hurt. Vehicle production has been the most dynamic major Brazilian industry. Shifting emphasis to other sectors should involve, in principle, no long-term problems, but short-term dislocations are inevitable, since so much of greater São Paulo industrialization constitutes the backward and forward linkages to auto production and maintenance. Slowing the auto boom will also frustrate those upper- middle-income consumers who see the private car as the sign of success and the key to physical mobility. And the latter is an understandable goal in a country as huge as Brazil. The government's striking unwillingness in 1974–75 promptly to pass through to consumers the full import cost of petroleum (and to slow down steel imports) showed that it was aware of the economic and politico-psychological effects of choking off the auto boom. That choice was finally made in 1975, *faute de mieux*. Frustration will undoubtedly grow among many who otherwise would be the regime's most logical supporters. It will be necessary to find other less import-intensive forms of consumption to satisfy them.

A Drag from Regional Inequalities? Finally, what of the enormous and growing regional disparities? Could the notorious lag of the Northeast, with its 30 million inhabitants, endanger Brazil's domestic growth rate.[10] Not directly. All the economies of scale favor the

---

[10] For a survey which is critical of government policies for their effects on urban populations, see D. E. Goodman, "The Brazilian Economic 'Miracle' and Regional Policy: Some Evidence from the Urban Northeast," *Journal of Latin American Studies*, vol. 8, no. 1 (May 1976), pp. 1-27. The most up-to-date

Center-South, which has created a dynamic sub-national economy fully the equivalent of the entire Argentine. Any Brazilian military officer ought to be deeply disturbed over the long-term geopolitical implications of these accelerating regional disparities within Brazil. Over a five-year projection, however, there is no reason to believe that the appalling misery of the backward regions will hold back the national economy. Nor does the potential for opposition in these areas appear sufficient to frighten Brasília into diverting significant funds toward low-yielding public investment schemes. The growing disillusion over the poorly conceived and badly planned Transamazon Highway underscores this point. Even a repeat of that kind of monumental project, hardly to be ruled out in the Brazil of Brasília (but unlikely given the Geisel government's style and thought thus far), would probably not divert large resources. It is worth remembering that much of the money for the Transamazon was diverted from federal funds originally earmarked for another project (SUDENE).

Conclusion. To sum up Brazil's economic prospects, the country's natural resources and demonstrated macro-management skills provide powerful assets for the near-term (that is, five years). Not least important is the highly centralized and sophisticated set of policy instruments under control of the federal government. The command capacity over the financial system and the public sector (both fiscal policy and the operations of state enterprises) is one of the most effective in the developing world and the equivalent of that in several industrial nations. In short, the Brazilian government's ability to direct the economy is far greater than it was a decade ago. My projections assume that over the next five years the Brazilian government will neither dismantle nor neglect to use this formidable apparatus for maintaining growth.

The Outlook for Domestic Politics

It is now more than a decade since a military-led conspiracy overthrew President João Goulart. Despite frequent predictions that the new government would prove inherently unstable, the Brazilian military and their civilian collaborators have succeeded in creating a notably resilient system of authoritarian government.[11] Is it likely to survive

---

survey is Roberto Cavalcanti de Albuquerque, "Nordeste: o Desenvolvimento Recente e a Estratégia do II PND," paper delivered at the meeting of the Sociedade Brasileira para o Progresso da Ciência in Brasília, July 1976.

[11] There are a rapidly growing number of studies of Brazil's political system as it was altered after 1964. My earlier article was an attempt to put those changes

the next five years? To answer requires a brief analysis of the system's recent evolution.

The Troubled Experiment in "Decompression." The experience of President Geisel's experiment in controlled "decompression" illustrates both the strength of the authoritarian elements in the system and the inherent limits to its potential liberalization. In the early months of the effort, in 1974, there was much discussion of how the liberalizers, presumably led by General Golbery, would need time to build a base of support among the principal army commanders. That, in turn, could only occur as the government was able to appoint its own regional commanders in the course of normal rotation. Observers who were optimistic about the prospects for "decompression" and who believed there was a good chance that the new president would pursue it vigorously, pointed to the arrival of the new second army commander in São Paulo, General Ednardo d'Avila Mello, as a sign of an impending shift away from the notoriously hard-line policies of his predecessor, General Humberto Souza Mello, an outspoken apologist for repression.

Only eighteen months later, many of these observers described General d'Avila as even worse than General Souza. The sensational death of Vladimir Herzog in October 1975 indicated the impunity with which the army-controlled security apparatus in São Paulo believed it could still operate. The President was able to force General d'Avila to resign in January. On first glance Geisel's action seemed not a repudiation of the repressive apparatus, but rather the jettisoning of a viceroy who had allowed ill-timed and repeated excesses to provoke unusually widespread condemnation. Through the first half of 1976, however, official torture apparently became less frequent. At the same time the Geisel government, like its predecessors, has resorted to cassations (an Anglicized version of the Portuguese term) and suspensions of political rights in order to discipline the congressional opposition and resolve local political disputes. The thought of a return to *habeas corpus* or a repeal of the Fifth Institutional Act seems unrealistic in the light of the Geisel government's continued reliance on arbitrary rule.

into historical perspective: "Politics and Economic Policy Making in Authoritarian Brazil, 1937-1971," in Stepan, ed., *Authoritarian Brazil*, pp. 3-46. The most satisfactory book-length studies are Ronald M. Schneider, *The Political System of Brazil: Emergence of a "Modernizing" Authoritarian Regime, 1964-1970* (New York: Columbia University Press, 1971); Georges-André Fiechter, *Brazil since 1964: Modernization under a Military Régime* (New York: John Wiley, 1975), which first appeared in French in 1972, and Celso Lafer, *O sistema político brasileiro* (São Paulo: Editora Perspectiva, 1975).

Key Government Weakness: Inability To Win Free Elections. Why this outcome? The process is too complex for adequate analysis here, but it is sufficient to say that any significant "opening" of the system is bound to threaten its very foundation. Why? Because the dominant force in the government—the military—can only maintain its position by the dual strategy of cooptation and authoritarian control. Without the latter, the former loses an important dimension. And without the threat—and on occasion the application—of repressive measures, the opposition would soon seriously threaten the government itself.

The Brazilian authoritarian political model, which has survived too long to be regarded as simply an ad hoc or make-shift structure, depends not only on arbitrary control, but also upon a skillful manipulation of the civilian political elite. Both of the officially sanctioned political parties (Aliança Renovadora Nacional, or ARENA, and Movimento Democrático Brasileiro, or MDB) are subject to constantly changing rules, both written and unwritten, which make sustained political organizing difficult and sometimes dangerous. Yet a surprisingly large number of would-be civilian politicians continue to come forward. There is even a new generation of bright young figures in both parties (although more in the MDB) whose experience of public life is entirely post-1964. The fact is that the hope of exercising political influence, even among many of the government's strongest critics, has remained alive in the civilian sector. It is impossible to understand the operation—and the resiliency—of Brazil's authoritarian system without keeping this factor in mind.

From the beginning of its direct intervention in 1964, the military has struggled with the problem of finding acceptable civilian politicians who could win elections, and the freer the elections, the greater the difficulty. None of the authoritarian governments since 1964 has been able to win a viable majority in a truly open election. In 1970 President Médici, for example, whom many foreign and domestic observers regarded as very popular, presided over the most blatantly manipulated elections of the last decade. The overwhelming victories for ARENA that year evidently convinced government strategists that they were at last beginning to find their long-sought civilian political base.

Subsequent elections, under freer conditions, shattered those illusions. The MDB's sweep in the November 1974 polling for the Congress startled even that party's most ebullient optimists. The prospects for the opposition seem equally bright over the next few years, even though the freedom of maneuver may not equal that of

1974, which included free access to television for the campaign. Then in 1978 will come the election of state governors, which is to be by direct popular vote, according to the constitution. Opposition victories in those elections could constitute a serious political threat to the leaders who still claim to speak in the name of the "Revolution." The government's only consolation over the near term is that the president to be elected in 1979 will be chosen by the present Congress, which includes an ARENA majority in both houses.

What Limits to MDB Growth? Is it likely that the Geisel government will allow the opposition to continue making such electoral gains? Why should we expect the higher military to accept the possibility of the opposition winning a majority in the next congressional elections and thereby being in a position to choose the new president in 1985?

The government's strategy is difficult to predict at this juncture. But the tone of MDB militancy that prevailed in the 1974 elections (criticizing the government for massive failures in social justice and human rights) seems fundamentally incompatible with the authoritarian views that have remained strong within the Geisel regime. As careful research on those elections has shown, the MDB rapidly developed appeal as a genuine opposition party.[12] Intimidated by the resurgence of torture and congressional cassations, however, the MDB entered 1976 far more defensively. During 1975 the Justice Ministry had increased its drumfire of propaganda about the "subversive threat," attributing MDB success to Communist manipulation. The most easily imagined scenario for a government move to tame the MDB at the polls would be a return to the Médici-style manipulation of 1969–70. That would not need to involve a suspension of Congress, as had happened in the 1968 crisis, although any major government purge of the MDB ranks (by cassation and suspension of political rights) might well provoke a party boycott. To summarize, the Geisel government has taken its political option, with the "hard line" (however archaic that term) retaining a veto power over the efforts of the liberalizing reformers. That trend will probably prevail for the remaining years of the Geisel presidency (his successor is to be inaugurated in March 1980).

Many unforeseen developments could intervene. Although apparently in good health and known for his penchant for work, General Geisel is, after all, sixty-seven years old. If he were to fall seriously

---

[12] Bolivar Lamounier and Fernando Henrique Cardoso, eds., *Os partidos e as eleições no Brasil* (Rio de Janeiro: Editora Paz e Terra, 1975).

ill or die, it would undoubtedly provoke a serious political crisis, since the constitutional Vice President, General Adalberto Pereira dos Santos, is two years older than Geisel and not considered a viable successor. To choose a new president on urgent notice could greatly exacerbate tensions within the officer corps, as happened in the succession crisis of 1969.

Stacking the Odds against Would-be Insurrectionaries. Both the U.S. and Brazilian governments have given much thought to the possibility of an armed insurrection. In fact, the armed revolutionary option has been attempted in Brazil. The revolutionary left tested the government by kidnapping the U.S. ambassador in 1969. The savage reaction, after ransoming the prisoners for the ambassador's release, signalled the beginning of an all-out offensive by the security interrogators.

Subsequently the underground challenged the government across the board, and was ignominiously defeated. Why? First, the government has had a far greater capacity to monitor all opposition activities than anyone would have predicted in 1964. The communications network of the federal government has grown enormously: teletype, satellite-aided links, microwave-assisted long distance telephone, and so on. With a computer bank of dossiers, the security authorities are able to maintain an extremely effective nationwide watch on suspects. Their efficiency makes the U.S. law enforcement structure look weak and archaic by comparison, even leaving aside the limits created by our commitment to safeguarding constitutional rights.

Second, the federal government has succeeded in greatly centralizing control over the security forces. The steady erosion of federalism since 1964 has nowhere been more marked than in the fight against "subversion." All the state secretaries of security are now under federal direction—meaning, in effect, under the military high command. In any large bureaucracy, such as the Brazilian security structure, there are bound to be cases of insubordination, deception, and oversight. But it is utterly naive to think that Brasília is less well informed about police and military interrogation methods (and their latest application) than the scores of journalists, churchmen, and foreign academics who can always bring the inquiring visitor up to date.

Third, the truth is that torture has proved to be a valuable instrument of intelligence gathering and a potent weapon for maintaining social control. It continues because those in control of the highest levels of government believe that at times it is indispensable. Middle-class observers from democratic societies too often fail to appreciate the enormously inhibiting effect of the threat of prolonged physical abuse. Recent history has produced few heroes from among the prisoners delivered into the hands of the torturers. Electric shocks, beatings, and abuse of family and colleagues have all helped generate the flood of information that has led police and military squads to one terrorist hide-out after another. The "big three" of the armed opposition—Carlos Marighela, Joaquim Ferreira Lima, and Carlos Lamarca—were all hunted down with the help of information gathered by the torturers. I was informed in mid-1974 that of the former Brazilian political prisoners who had been ransomed in return for kidnapped foreign diplomats there were twenty-four who had reentered Brazil clandestinely, and of those the government security forces could already account for twenty-three bodies. Furthermore, the huge surveillance apparatus has made it virtually impossible to organize any extensive armed opposition. Wire-tapping, letter-opening, and recourse to a vast number of informers makes every political gesture by more than a handful of persons known to the government. Although inefficiencies undoubtedly occur, the machine has left few Brazilians in any doubt that the odds are overwhelmingly in its favor.

Along with the stick has come the carrot. The rapid economic growth in recent years has created great prosperity and power for the Brazilian elite. The Brazilian universities, to take one example, have been greatly strengthened in the last few years, although still suffering from serious problems of structure and funding. The Brazilian government has largely succeeded in reversing the brain drain which occurred in the 1964-70 period, in contrast to the continuing hemorrhage from authoritarian Chile, Uruguay, and Argentina. For Brazilians willing to accommodate themselves to the political realities, the rewards can be great, both personally and in institutional accomplishments in their field. The effect is strongest among the young of the middle and upper social sectors—the very strata from which the armed opposition had once recruited most successfully.

It is worth remembering also that Brazil has no major ethnic, linguistic, or regional cleavages that might facilitate the mobilization of an armed opposition. Despite the vast differences in income (and therefore social welfare), the Brazilian population is relatively homogenous. That is a further asset for the authoritarian regime.

Recent history shows that the odds are against an armed opposition attacking a determined government fully prepared to use all authoritarian methods in controlling its own people. Colonial cases, such as Algeria, are obviously different. The apparent exception is

21

Vietnam, which can only be explained by a careful historical analysis of the long French administration and its aftermath. The apparent ease with which the Brazilian government has snuffed out centers of armed opposition in São Paulo, Paraná, and Amazonas in the last five years seems to confirm the lesson for Brazil.

Long-term Explosive Potential? What about the longer term? Could the continuing repression store up a potential explosion? No historian would want to rule out such a possibility, but there are many factors militating against it in the next few years, not least the character of Brazilian society and culture. The heavily personalistic and patrimonial ethos tends to blur lines of potential social conflict, at least in the eyes of the Brazilians at the bottom. The effect is to retard the development of class consciousness in the lower sectors and diffuse any sense of group identification. Although it would be dangerous to overestimate this factor, it does constitute an asset for the regime.

Finally, might serious economic trouble erode the government's de facto legitimacy and thereby help the opposition to mobilize? Obviously that is possible. The economic slowdown in the second half of 1974 undoubtedly swayed some votes toward the MDB in the congressional elections. But is it not reasonable to assume that the military would tighten their political control in such a crisis? Any prudent observer would have to conclude that the political initiative will continue to lie with the government over the next five years.

The Future Evolution of Brazil's International Relations

A projection of Brazil's international relations can best be framed around the following set of assumptions.[13] The concluding section will discuss their implications for U.S.-Brazilian relations.

Economic Considerations and Brazil's Foreign Policy Priorities. Brazil must maintain vigorous export growth, as well as maximize the avail-

---

[13] The best introduction to an understanding of Brazil's current international role is Brady B. Tyson, "Brazil" in Harold Eugene Davis and Larman C. Wilson, eds., *Latin American Foreign Policies: An Analysis* (Baltimore: The Johns Hopkins University Press, 1975), pp. 221-258, which includes extensive discussion of the relevant bibliography. For a Brazilian view of Brazil's post-1964 foreign policy, see Carlos Estevam Martins, "A Evolução da política externa brasileira na década 64/74," *Estudos CEBRAP*, no. 12 (April-May-June 1975), pp. 53-98. The most authoritative analyses of the current context of inter-American relations are the chapters by Riordan Roett, C. Fred Bergsten and Roger Hansen in *The Americas in a Changing World* (New York: Quadrangle, 1975).

ability of foreign technology, capital, and fuel.[14] This will require such ideological pragmatism as has been evident in the sugar deals with the U.S.S.R. and the (partially) oil-influenced early recognition of the Angolan MPLA. The urgent need for oil also led Brazil, like many other less-developed countries (LDCs), to change its Middle East policy dramatically. A continued pro-Arab stance, despite its meager practical returns to date, can be expected over the near term.

The search for other sources of foreign fuel will also strongly influence Brazilian foreign policy. Hydroelectric power is Brazil's most important substitute for the lacking fossil fuels, yet its exploitation requires skillful diplomacy because the rivers of greatest potential are located on the southwestern and southern and western borders. The giant Itaipú dam complex on the Paraguayan frontier, already under construction, involves a joint Brazilian-Paraguayan effort that will make electricity Paraguay's most important export. The national security implications for Brazil in having such a major power source across an international frontier are obvious.[15]

The search for energy has also led Brazil to pursue successful negotiations for oil and natural gas concessions in Bolivia. Unconfirmed but highly plausible reports point to Brazilian collaboration in the coup which brought General Hugo Banzer to power in 1971. Bolivian internal politics will grow more important to Brazil as the level of energy exports to Brazil increases. Over the next five years, however, the Bolivian connection will probably be far less vital than the Paraguayan. Moreover, direct intervention in Bolivia would also be much more difficult logistically than in Paraguay.

The drive for export markets represents a further preoccupation. It will probably mean more tied sales of primary products, such as the agreement to sell iron ore to Japan in return for a wide range of technological investments in Brazil. More dramatic is the 1975 accord with West Germany to exchange natural uranium from Brazil's rich reserves for advanced nuclear technology from Bonn. In this

---

14 The economic considerations behind official Brazilian foreign policy thinking were clearly indicated in Chancellor Azeredo da Silveira's speech in London in October 1975, reprinted in Ministério das Relações Exteriores, Resenha de Política Exterior do Brasil, vol. 2, no. 7 (October-December 1975), pp. 52-56.

15 For an analysis of the complex legal and administrative basis for the huge Itaipú project, see José Costa Cavalcanti, "A Itaipú binacional—um exemplo de cooperação internacional na América Latina," Revista de Administração Pública, vol. 10, no. 1 (January-March 1976), pp. 19-68. Brazil has carefully prepared the way for its borderland hydro-electric projects by getting prior agreements, in principle, to multi-country activities, as in the Treaty of the Prata Basin (1969) and the Asunción Declaration on the Use of International Rivers (1971), both of which were signed by Argentina, Bolivia, Brazil, Paraguay, and Uruguay.

23

case, energy needs became combined with strategic ambitions to strengthen Brazil's defiance of the strong U.S. effort against the agreement.[16]

One area in which Brazilian trade policy will grow more aggressive is the area of manufactured products, Brazil's fastest growing export during the last several years. Having built the largest industrial park in the developing world, Brazil will be in a strong position to push sale of Brazilian finished goods abroad. For example, an absolute decline in Brazilian auto production was averted last year only by increased exports, which compensated for the drop in domestic auto sales. Brazil has already encountered discrimination against manufactured exports from the United States (shoes) and the European Economic Community (finished textiles) and will fight such treatment strongly. This will make her an increasingly prominent voice among LDCs—such as the Group of Twenty-four—attacking the trade policies of the industrial nations.

Diversification of the Lines of Foreign Economic Dependence. Brazil has been attempting to increase its bargaining power by developing new trade relationships through shrewd marketing of primary products—especially minerals and agricultural goods (Brazil became the world's second leading exporter of both sugar and soybeans in 1975). Diversification can also mean reduced political vulnerability, as Brazil continues to work its way out of its forty-year heavy reliance on trade and capital ties with the United States. The most dramatic evidence of this process is what has happened with coffee. In the early 1960s Brazil depended upon coffee exports for more than half the country's foreign exchange earnings, with the largest percentage coming from the United States. In 1974, by contrast, coffee accounted for only 12.6 percent of export earnings, less than sugar (15.8 percent). Bypassing the United States for advanced nuclear technology is another example of diversification. Despite heavy pressure on both West Germany and Brazil, normally considered among the most responsive of our allies, the United States failed to stop the historic 1975 nuclear agreement. Brazil's drive to diversify its foreign economic relations may well intensify over the next five years.

From Third to Second-Rank International Power Status. Brazil's ambitions for such an improved world position date back to the country's

---

[16] For an excellent analysis of the 1975 agreement for West Germany to supply Brazil with nuclear technology and equipment, see Norman Gall, "Atoms for Brazil, Dangers for All," *Foreign Policy*, no. 23 (Summer 1976), pp. 155-201.

angry withdrawal from the League of Nations in 1926 when other Latin American delegations failed to support its bid for a seat on the League of Nations Council. Brazilian rivalry with Argentina for Latin American preeminence goes back to the mid-nineteenth century, but in the last decade Brazil has clearly established a lead, much to the frustration of the Argentines. Since the Second World War, when alliance with the United States was parlayed into significant military and economic aid, Brazil has chosen de facto to operate bilaterally in important hemispheric dealings with the United States, although usually observing the forms of the Organization of American States. Brazil paid little attention to the supposedly multilateral machinery of the Alliance for Progress, for example, and the Kennedy and Johnson administrators of the U.S. Agency for International Development (AID) accommodated Brazil's bilateral approach. The U.S.-Brazil "memorandum of understanding," (more on this later) signed in Brasília on February 21, 1976, is a dramatic reaffirmation of this approach.

On the world scene, Brazil will continue to seek the best of both worlds—asserting leadership of the LDCs while also aspiring to possible OECD membership, as predicted by Ambassador Lincoln Gordon.[17] In comparative terms Brazil cannot hope to rival the financial or military power of an Iran, although its industrial capacity will be far superior. On the other hand, Brazil may well look stronger overall by 1981 than Indonesia or Nigeria (both with oil).[18] It is worth reemphasizing that Brazil's Center-South *region* has already emerged as more than the equal in production and population of any Latin American country except Mexico. Overall, Brazil's production now places it as the world's ninth largest nation in GDP.

The Low Probability of Military Conflict on Brazil's Borders. Brazil's rapid economic growth, along with its militantly anti-Communist ideological posture (at least within South America), has led to much speculation about possible Brazilian expansionist designs.[19] Economic

---

[17] Lincoln Gordon, "Brazil's Future World Role," *Orbis*, vol. 16, no. 3 (Fall 1972).

[18] One of the principal themes of official Brazilian foreign policy statements in recent years has been the need to maintain flexibility in international relations. The classic statement of that position came in a speech in 1971 by João Augusto de Araújo Castro, then Brazilian ambassador to the United States, under the title of "The United Nations and the Freezing of the International Power Structure," and was reprinted in *International Organization*, vol. 26, no. 1 (Winter 1972), pp. 158-166.

[19] For the prognosis of one specialist who expects an increase in competition, if not in conflict, among South American countries, see Alexandre de S. C. Barros, "The New Role of the State and International Politics in South America," paper prepared for the meeting of the International Studies Association in Toronto, February 1976.

penetration of bordering countries, especially in the Rio de la Plata region, will undoubtedly increase. But for the following reasons one can regard the potential for Brazilian-initiated military conflict as low.

First, the Brazilian army does not have enough ammunition to engage in large-scale combat for any extended period. Part of present supplies comes from Belgium and resupply would require an emergency airlift, barring appeal to some other source. Lacking a domestic source of supply of all varieties, and lacking long-distance military air cargo capacity, any Brazilian army units crossing a border would find themselves running out of some forms of ammunition within weeks. It should be added that plans for the creation of an expanded Brazilian munitions industry were announced in 1975. When the plants become operational, presumably within the next five years, dependence on foreign ammunition will no longer be the same inhibiting factor.

Second, Brazil's capacity to supply combat forces on any of its vast borders, except in the Plata basin, is extremely limited. To mount and maintain an incursion into Bolivia, Peru, Colombia, Venezuela, or the three northern neighbors of Guyana, Surinam and French Guiana would present gigantic logistical problems. The Brazilian military lacks the air cargo transport and helicopters needed to make such incursions anything more than border skirmishes. The army's out-of-date armor is maneuvered only infrequently, and then on the relatively good roads near the principal garrisons. Moving it great distances would appear impossible. It should be remembered that all of these borders (excluding the Plata region) are at least a thousand miles (two thousand in several cases) from any significant troop concentrations and even farther from the industrial heartland.

Third, even if the logistical capacity existed, the Brazilian army has *not* been trained to be a mobile national fighting force.[20] Enlisted men are generally recruited from the locality where they serve and many continue to live with their families. There is little experience with long-distance maneuvers. Practice in deploying large numbers of combat troops over distant terrain has simply not been acquired.

Fourth, for Brazil to undertake a major military action on the company's borders would render the government much more vulnerable to opposition back home than it would be in peacetime. Because the authoritarian regime depends directly on its formidable security apparatus, largely directed and staffed by the military, to divert the

---

[20] Alfred Stepan, *The Military in Politics, Changing Patterns in Brazil* (Princeton: Princeton University Press, 1971).

26

army to foreign adventures could seriously weaken basic security and thereby endanger the survival of the military government itself. Granted the unlikelihood of Brazil launching an attack across its own borders, might the initiative come from the country's neighbors? The same logistical problems would certainly bedevil the Venezuelans, Peruvians, Colombians, or Bolivians, whom few observers would (in any case) regard as likely to invade Brazil. The most sensitive region is the Plata basin, an area of armed conflict from the colonial era through the Paraguayan War (1865–70). Brazil's southernmost state, Rio Grande do Sul, hosts far more Brazilian troops than any other state. Deep and historic military suspicions surround Brazilian relations with Argentina. Even in World War II, when the Axis threat to Brazil's northeastern coast was at its height, the United States had great difficulty convincing the Brazilian military to shift any troops from their watch on the Argentine border.[21] One still finds frequent speculation in the press of both countries about supposedly growing tensions. One can measure Argentine fears of growing Brazilian power by reading such journals as *Estrategia*, which in recent years featured numerous highly agitated warnings from Argentine military officers about Brazil's geopolitical ambitions in Latin America.[22] Notwithstanding this background of suspicion, both Argentine and Brazilian postures are essentially defensive. The deep political divisions within Argentina, which are fully mirrored in the military, make any Argentine initiative all the less likely.

What about Uruguay or Paraguay? In the former case, Brazil has long exercised a very strong economic tutelage and it is worth remembering that Uruguay owes its existence to Britain's desire to create a buffer state between the two major Plata powers—Argentina and Brazil. As long as Uruguay maintains an authoritarian government so close in ideology to Brazil's, there is little threat in either direction.[23] The security forces of the two countries already cooperate closely. As for possible border conflict, Uruguay lacks the capacity to challenge the large Brazilian forces across the frontier, should any misguided soldier or politician entertain aggressive designs.

Paraguay constitutes an even less credible military threat to Brazil. The danger there lies in the possibility of internal instability—

---

[21] Details may be found in Frank D. McCann, Jr., *The Brazilian-American Alliance, 1937-45* (Princeton: Princeton University Press, 1973).

[22] Examples of such articles may be found in *Estrategia*, no. 28 (May-June 1974) and nos. 37/38 (November-December/January-February 1975/76). An article in the latter came in for bemused comment in the *Folha de São Paulo*, June 24, 1976.

[23] For a representative statement by the Uruguayan foreign minister, see the report in *Jornal do Brasil*, June 16, 1976.

perhaps following Stroessner's demise, when that occurs—which might draw Brazil into conflict, first to safeguard the electric power supply from Itaipú and second to block any extension of Argentine influence. The greatest potential for conflict on Brazil's borders exists with Paraguay, and both Brazilians and Argentines regard Asunción as an important capital to watch.

Unlikelihood of a Radical Domestic Political Shift. The potential for successful insurgency in Brazil over the next few years seems low. And there is little reason to expect any Soviet intervention, barring a protracted civil war or a power vacuum otherwise created. Even given such a dramatic development, we might expect extreme caution from the Union of Soviet Socialist Republics. The fate of the Allende regime in 1973 showed how quickly "the socialist camp" can write off a South American regime they once regarded with interest and sympathy.

Implications for U.S.-Brazilian Relations

The pattern of factors that will dominate U.S. relations with Brazil over the next five years has been indicated, implicitly, in the preceding sections.[24] They are as follows:

Pro-American Bias in Brazilian Ruling Circles. Here I assume that a military-dominated government (granting nothing more than relatively minor concessions to civilian politicians) will prevail until 1981. The military officer corps continues to show a pro-U.S. bias, which has deep historical roots in the World War II experience. Although the Brazilian officers involved in those years have retired, the extensive U.S. Military Assistance Program (MAP) of the postwar years brought many younger officials to the United States for training. Between 1952 and 1969, 5,469 Brazilian military "students" received

---

[24] In an earlier article analyzing U.S. policy toward Brazil, I cited some of the relevant sources: "United States Policy toward Brazil: Assumptions and Options," in Ronald G. Hellman & H. Jon Rosenbaum, eds., *Latin American International Affairs Series*, vol. 1: "Latin America: The Search for a New International Role" (New York: Sage Publications, 1975). Among the important recent analyses of U.S.-Brazilian relations are Carlos Estevam Martins, "Brazil and the United States from the 1960's to the 1970's," in Julio Cotler and Richard R. Fagen, eds., *Latin America and the United States: The Changing Political Realities* (Stanford: Stanford University Press, 1974); Peter D. Bell, "Brazilian-American Relations," in Riordan Roett, ed., *Brazil in the Sixties* (Nashville: Vanderbilt University Press, 1972); Roger W. Fontaine, *Brazil and the United States* (Washington, D.C.: American Enterprise Institute for Public Policy Research, 1974).

MAP-sponsored training in the United States.[25] Even if we acknowledge that the effect of such exposure is difficult to assess, the net consequence has undoubtedly been to promote a continuing identification of Brazilian and U.S. interests. It has often been predicted that the Brazilian military might exhibit a nationalist (that is, an anti-U.S.) reaction, but the reality has proved different. The military "nationalists" have suffered repeated reversals, usually resulting in their being purged to the reserve, where their political influence is minimal. The best-known example was General Albuquerque Lima, who was forced from power (minister of the interior) in 1970. The military hierarchy has proved adept at neutralizing internal dissension, especially from the nationalists, as the 1974–75 debate over the risk contracts for international oil companies illustrated.

The past record would lead one to predict that the pro-U.S. faction will continue to prevail. This is not to say that its relative strength may not decline, or that on specific issues, especially economic policy, there will not be a divergence of interests. But the military, and therefore the government, will seek to remain close to the United States politically, ideologically, and militarily.[26]

Economic Issues Divisive in U.S.-Brazilian Relations. Conflict should be expected over trade and private U.S. investment.

(1) *Trade.* In trade, Brazil will continue to furnish export competition to the United States in several important primary product markets such as soybeans. The U.S. Department of Agriculture ruefully noted in 1975 that Brazilian soybeans proved to be of higher quality than the U.S. variety and that the Brazilians showed unexpected expertise in marketing their beans.[27] There will also be the long-familiar struggles over the price paid by U.S. consumers for Brazilian coffee (through international coffee agreements, such as the one negotiated in London in 1975) and the amount of processed (soluble) coffee allowed into the U.S. market.

An area of greater tension will be U.S. policy toward Brazilian manufactured exports. Hard-pressed U.S. shoe manufacturers forced the Treasury to invoke a seldom-observed law of the 1890s which

---

[25] U.S. Congress, House, Subcommittee on National Security Policy and Scientific Developments of the Committee on Foreign Affairs, *Hearings on Military Assistance Training*, 91st Congress, 2nd session, October 6, 7, 8, December 8 and 15, 1970 (Washington, D.C.: U.S. Government Printing Office, 1970), p. 14.

[26] An informative story in 1975 by Marvine Howe discussed the implications for U.S.-Brazilian relations of Brazil's attempt to diversify her dependence on foreign help: *New York Times*, July 2, 1975.

[27] *Wall Street Journal*, July 3, 1975; *Business Week*, July 26, 1976.

requires countervailing duties on imports from countries that subsidize export of the products in question. In September 1974 a duty was applied to Brazilian shoes. Although the amount was small, the Brazilian government protested vigorously, arguing that the U.S. action made a mockery of past U.S. appeals to rely on "trade not aid." The incident also fed long-standing export pessimism (the argument being that the industrial economies will never admit competition of their own manufactured exports in *their* markets) endemic among an older generation of Brazilian economists and intellectuals. Yet the younger policy makers are more robust, and shoes are likely to be only the opening round in a series of battles prompted by threatened U.S. producers and their employees' union representatives.

(2) *U.S. private investment.* U.S. private investment in Brazil is an area of economic relations where potential conflict over the next five years is difficult to evaluate. The United States will remain the largest single source of accumulated direct investment, although Japanese and West European investors will continue to prove aggressive and resourceful. As the radical critics have often pointed out, foreign investors control many of the most dynamic sectors of Brazilian industry, such as vehicles, household appliances, and pharmaceuticals. Might this large investment, largely U.S. in origin, fall hostage to a nationalist backlash in Brazil? Such an occurrence could only come as the consequence of a basic shift in Brazilian domestic politics. Such a prospect seems unlikely over the next five years.

But the issue area is so sensitive that the points of potential conflict should be examined with care. First, the Brazilian government might react strongly to the pricing policies of U.S. multinationals —drawing, for example, on the evidence generated by the Senate Foreign Relations Subcommittee investigating multinational corporations.[28] Controlling the oligopolistic behavior of U.S. firms would be within the power of the Brazilian government, given the resolve. Whether the U.S. government would commit its prestige to defending discriminatory pricing policies by U.S. firms would depend on the ideological leanings of the administration then in power in Washington.

More difficult, however, may be profit remittances and payments for royalties and technology. These have been a special target of nationalist critics, who have stressed the balance-of-payments burden

---

[28] Richard S. Newfarmer and Willard F. Mueller, U.S. Congress, Senate, Subcommittee on Multinational Corporations of the Committee on Foreign Relations, *Multinational Corporations in Brazil and Mexico: Structural Sources of Economic and Noneconomic Power*, 94th Congress, 1st session (Washington, D.C.: U.S. Government Printing Office, 1975).

of servicing the private foreign account. For the decade from 1960 through 1969, for example, remittance by U.S. firms exceeded the inflow of new U.S. investment capital into Brazil.[29] But *is* this the most important measure of the economic impact of direct foreign investment? Strictly speaking, such data tell us only that repatriated returns on *all* past investment happened to total more than new commitments made in the designated period. There is no necessary connection between the two. Profit remittances and new direct foreign investment are influenced by many separate factors, although the prospect of remittable profit and other payments (for royalties, technical services, and so on), along with eventual repatriation, is obviously a prime consideration in businessmen's decisions to commit first-time or additional capital.

Yet there is no denying that the difference between remittances (with other payments and capital repatriation) and new capital inflow *does* measure the net balance-of-payments impact of direct foreign investments in the strict accounting sense. A further consideration, inherently immeasurable but nonetheless important, is the contribution of direct foreign investments to creating domestic capacity that will substitute for items previously imported, thereby saving foreign exchange. If the net private account should turn sharply negative, Brazilian policy makers might clamp down on remittances or repatriation.[30] Such action was threatened by President Vargas in 1952, although it was never carried out.[31] In 1961, however, the pendulum swung back toward the nationalists, who pushed through the Brazilian Congress a law limiting remittances to 10 percent per year, to be calculated on a base excluding any reinvested profits. The law provoked howls of protest from the U.S. embassy and U.S. investors, but it was never tested in practice because President Goulart, in grave political danger, procrastinated two years in issuing the enabling decree to put the law in operation. By that time—early 1964— Goulart was only a few months away from being deposed. The sharp drop in new direct foreign investments which had occurred between 1961 and 1964 may have been due more to the protracted economic

---

[29] U.S. Congress, Senate, Subcommittee on Western Hemisphere Affairs of the Committee on Foreign Relations, *United States Policies and Programs in Brazil*, 92nd Congress, 1st session, May 4, 5, and 11, 1971 (Washington, D.C.: U.S. Government Printing Office, 1971), p. 215.

[30] In 1974, for example, the net impact of 115 multinational firms on the Brazilian balance of payments was negative in the amount of $1.73 billion. These data were calculated by the Ministério do Planejamento and published in *Jornal do Brasil*, May 30, 1976.

[31] For details see Thomas E. Skidmore, *Politics in Brazil, 1930-1964* (New York: Oxford University Press, 1967), pp. 99-100.

slowdown and disorganization, along with the growing political instability, than to the 1961 law. One of the earliest steps taken by the new military-dominated government in 1964 was to repeal that law and arrange a more liberal one, which imposes a graduated tax on remittances.

Could the pendulum swing again? It could, but only as part of a more general swing toward economic nationalism. Such a shift by the present military-dominated government appears unlikely. The 1975 decision to open Brazil to risk contracts with foreign oil firms (reached only after a long debate) was further evidence of the pragmatic views of the officers in charge, even in an area long regarded as sacrosanct by nationalists. This is not to say that military officers and like-minded civilian policy makers will not continue to protect the enormous state sector (electric power, transportation, communications, iron ore, the vast majority of oil) from incursions by private foreign interests. But there is little likelihood that over the next five years the government will suddenly change the rules on profit remittances or capital repatriation. The most plausible scenario for such action would be a balance-of-payments deficit so severe that the Brazilian government could not afford to worry about the efforts of emergency regulations on new direct foreign investments. But in that case direct foreign investments would undoubtedly be lagging anyway. Even in this case a short-term suspension of remittances and repatriation could meet the immediate crisis.

If we look ahead more than five years, it turns out that the servicing of direct foreign investments may prove a far more serious problem than in the short run. Unlike a loan, direct foreign investments constitute an open-ended, potentially unlimited base for future servicing. For this reason, Brazil, like other less-developed countries, can be expected to seek badly needed technology in forms *other* than direct foreign investments. Furthermore, Brazilians will probably become more concerned about the degree of foreign ownership of the dynamic private sector. The growth of the Brazilian state sector and of foreign enterprises continues to squeeze out Brazilian business. The Brazilian capitalist model lacks Brazilian capitalists. This situation is traceable to factors in the world economy as well as in Brazil, and nothing short of extreme government action is likely to alter it in the short run.

Over the longer term, however, the role of direct foreign investments may well decline in relative terms. Changes from the U.S. side could be important. Long past are the days, as in the 1950s, when the U.S. government preached the virtues of U.S. private investment as the cure for all the economic ills of the less-developed countries. Washington is now too worried about our own balance of payments (any new investment abroad is initially a balance-of-payments liability) and in any case is considerably more sophisticated than it used to be about the mixed effects of direct foreign investments in the developing world.

A relic of the earlier view is OPIC (Overseas Private Investment Corporation), the U.S.-government-backed insurance agency which covers U.S. private investors' risks overseas (against exchange controls, expropriation, and so on). OPIC coverage guarantees official U.S. involvement whenever (as defined by OPIC) an insured firm falls afoul of a host government. If a sharp nationalist swing should occur in Brazil, OPIC, and therefore the U.S. government, would have a large and immediate stake because Brazil is host to more OPIC-insured U.S. investment than any other country in the world. The potential political liability is obvious.

A final consideration from the U.S. standpoint is relevant for the longer term. Opinion in the United States may shift against direct foreign investment as the most effective (or profitable) form of private business commitment abroad.[32]

(3) *Foreign debt management*. Brazil's foreign debt grew at a staggering rate during 1974 and 1975 and by early 1976 Brazil was the largest single debtor nation (over $3 billion) in the loan portfolios of U.S. commercial banks, as well as being the principal borrower from the World Bank, where U.S. influence has remained strong. In this area Brazil would appear to have relatively little room for maneuver over the next year or two. The freewheeling confidence in international financial circles that characterized Delfim Neto's last few years is past, and the urgent need to maintain credit-worthiness abroad (especially in U.S. banking and government circles) is bound to act as a check on aspirations toward a policy more "independent" of the United States.

Brazil as a U.S. Ally in Latin American Relations but Otherwise Independent. Brazil has a long record of close alliance with the United States in hemispheric affairs, and this closeness can be expected to continue, especially in the political and ideological area. Indeed, the

---

[32] Robert Gilpin, "An Alternative Strategy to Foreign Investment," *Challenge*, vol. 18, no. 5 (November-December 1975). A number of recent studies by economists have concluded that overseas investment by United States-based firms may reduce U.S. labor's share of the national income and therefore are notably vulnerable to political attack by organized labor. The studies are discussed in a feature story in the *New York Times*, February 23, 1976.

February 1976 "Memorandum of Understanding" is a confirmation of the pattern. Collaboration may extend to working together in "destabilizing" South American regimes that both the United States and Brazil wish to topple or isolate. Brazilian penetration in the domestic politics of Uruguay has a long history, as to a lesser extent, has Brazilian penetration in Paraguay and Bolivia. It seems difficult to believe that Brazil did not play a role in the swings to the right in Bolivia in 1971 and Uruguay in 1973. At the least, Brazilian security forces have worked closely with their counterparts in bordering countries (especially Uruguay) to monitor and control movement of exiles, foreign agents, and all others considered worthy of government attention. Even with Chile, which has no common frontier with Brazil, a close relationship between the security apparatus existed from the moment of the 1973 coup against Allende, and there is evidence that private Brazilian interests (could Brasília fail to have been involved also?) [33] helped finance and advise the Chilean conspirators. In all these cases Brazil has been playing, from the U.S. standpoint, the role of a helpful ally ("continental gendarme," as Spanish-American critics call it) by pursuing political and ideological objectives which it shares with the United States. If my previous projections about Brazilian economic growth and political development prove correct, then we may expect this role to continue over the next five years.

One important qualification must be added. The swing to the right throughout South America in the last few years means that future opposition movements will be directed against regimes favored by the U.S. and Brazilian governments. Would Brazil intervene to stop a swing to the left in a bordering country? Given its relative military weakness, Brasília is likely to be cautious, but Paraguay may be the case to watch most closely. The U.S. intelligence and security community will undoubtedly continue to get information and close collaboration from Brazilian counterparts, but the ambitious "dirty tricks" (on the level of relentless detail revealed by Philip Agee and by recent congressional inquiries) will continue to be up to the United States.[34]

---

[33] A story by Marlise Simons on links between Brazilian private interests and the anti-Allende conspirators in Chile was published in the *Washington Post*, January 7, 1974.

[34] Philip Agee, *Inside the Company: CIA Diary* (Harmondsworth, England: Penguin, Ltd., 1975). A wealth of information on covert operations by the CIA in Chile is given in U.S. Congress, Senate, *Hearings before the Select Committee to Study Governmental Operations with Respect to Intelligence Activities of the United States Senate*, 94th Congress, 1st session, vol. 7: Covert Action, December 4 & 5, 1975 (Washington, D.C.: U.S. Government Printing Office, 1976).

On certain economic and geopolitical issues within the hemisphere, Brazilian and U.S. interests are more likely to diverge. The 200-mile territorial waters limit is an example. Although her fishing industry is far less developed than it might be, the Brazilian government's support for Ecuador and Peru in their dispute with the United States must be seen in the light of Brasília's ambitious plans for its own future industry. Nuclear power is another example. Brazil badly needs the fuel that nuclear reactors can provide. But her military (and many civilian) leaders also fear being left out in the nuclear race, especially considering that Argentina is the only other Latin American country with a cadre of sophisticated nuclear physicists. Brasília's refusal to sign the nuclear non-proliferation treaty and its multi-billion nuclear agreement with West Germany show the importance of both economic and geopolitical preoccupations in a vital policy area where intense U.S. pressure proved unavailing.[35] Although Argentina's current political and economic travail has gravely weakened that country's continental position, we must assume that within the next five years Buenos Aires will react strongly to Brazil's nuclear buildup, even though that buildup, at least as provided in the agreement with West Germany, includes no explicitly military components. United States policy makers ought to give thought (and they undoubtedly have already) to the implications of a nuclear dimension added to the historic Argentine-Brazilian rivalry. By 1981 the southern cone of South America may well have come close to matching the South Asian subcontinent and the Middle East as areas of nuclear confrontation in the developing world. The failure to gain Brazilian agreement to the first major U.S. effort to prevent this—the nuclear non-proliferation treaty—shows how very limited U.S. influence is likely to be.

Elsewhere in international politics, Brazil will become increasingly independent of the United States. There are powerful economic considerations behind this trend. It has already been felt in the U.N., where the Latin American votes were long assumed to be securely in the U.S. ambassador's pocket. The "Zionism as racism" resolution, which the United States fought so bitterly, gained Brazil's support, thereby continuing the country's pursuit of Arab favor in hope of cheaper oil, although Brazil's special sensitivity to any kind of "racism" created a special interest. Angola is another example. As the most powerful Portuguese-speaking nation and one with long

---

[35] Typical of the U.S. reaction was the New York Times editorial of June 13, 1975, entitled "Nuclear Madness."

historic ties to Angola, Brazil is in a position to wield considerable influence there. But Brasília has chosen to bet on the MPLA, which Kissinger and Ford battled so tenaciously. In the Third World, it thus appears Brazil will follow its own lights more and more. Brazil is currently supporting the OPEC cause, despite the enormous increase in its own oil bill, partly out of a belief that the country stands to gain greatly from future participation in such cartels.[36] In relations with the industrial nations, especially the EEC and Japan, Brazil's economic interests will often put it on the opposite side from the United States (that is, the side of the lesser developed countries) in international trade and financial negotiations.

Continued Potential for Human Rights Conflict with an Authoritarian Government in Brazil. The U.S. government has hardly been in the forefront of public protest over the authoritarian measures systematically employed by the Brazilian police and military since 1968. On the contrary, Kissinger's policy has been to subordinate the human rights question to what the secretary defines as other U.S. priorities. Kissinger's rush to identify U.S. interests with the Greek colonels has only been the most publicized example of this *Realpolitik*, not the only example. It was intense congressional pressure and wider diplomatic considerations that led Kissinger at the last minute to instruct Ambassador Moynihan to vote in favor of the 1975 U.N. resolution condemning the Chilean junta's massive violations of human rights.

In President Nixon's first year, before Kissinger achieved mastery over U.S. foreign policy, the U.S. government did show extreme displeasure with Brazil's authoritarian turn. The aid pipeline was virtually closed in fiscal year 1969, with total loans and grants dropping to only $30 million, compared to more than ten times that amount in fiscal year 1968 ($316.8 million). There were also behind-the-scenes protests to the Brazilian government over the crippling of most of the remaining democratic institutions (suspending the Congress, and so on) and the suppressing of civil rights. Subsequently a higher level of U.S. aid was resumed (the total reached $154.8 million in fiscal year 1970) and even the behind-the-scenes protests apparently died down. With Kissinger in full control, there has been little U.S. rocking of the Brazilian boat, despite the fact that

---

[36] Brazil's large reserve of bauxite nourishes the hope that Brazil might benefit from a cartel in that product, as outlined in C. Fred Bergsten, "A New OPEC in Bauxite," *Challenge*, vol. 19, no. 3 (July-August 1976).

torture has been amply documented by reliable international sources in Brazil since 1969.[37]

The ultimate test of U.S. policy in this area is torture of U.S. citizens in Brazil. The first unambiguous case (there were victims with dual U.S.-Brazilian citizenship earlier) came in September 1974, when Fred Morris, a former Methodist missionary, was arrested and physically assaulted (beatings, electric shocks) in the Brazilian Fourth Army installations in Recife. The U.S. Embassy reacted vigorously, all the more since U.S. officials had known Morris was under surveillance, had satisfied themselves he was involved in no anti-government activities, and had warned Brazilian authorities that the United States would take a strong interest if Morris were mistreated. His subsequent arrest and abuse was taken by our embassy as a direct challenge. Quick reaction by U.S. consular and embassy officials stopped the torture after a few days and led to Morris's release a few weeks later. It is a measure of the State Department's posture under Kissinger that the U.S. Embassy's recommendation for an extremely strong protest was accepted only reluctantly by the Department of State.[38]

What of U.S. official attitudes on human rights over the next five years? With Jimmy Carter's move into the White House in 1977, might U.S. policy toward an authoritarian government in Brazil change? [39] The first point to note is that U.S. government aid to Brazil is now minimal. In fiscal year 1974 it totalled only $69.9 million, of which $52.7 million was military aid. The latter might come under attack from a Carter administration, and to cut it off would be primarily a symbolic act. The U.S. military has been very closely tied to its Brazilian counterpart, and ending the military aid disbursements would not necessarily sever the service links, which exist on an exchange basis independent of AID budgets. To choke off the military supply line, on the other hand, would turn the Brazilian military

---

[37] The Department of International Affairs of the United States Catholic Conference, for example, issued a protest in mid-1970, as reported in *The National Catholic Reporter*, June 5, 1970. For details on documentation and protests by other groups, including a papal commission, see *The Sunday Times* (London), May 17, 1970. The most continuous reporting on torture in Brazil has come from Amnesty International, which published a worldwide survey of torture, with discussion of the Brazilian case: Amnesty International, *Report on Torture* (New York: Farrar, Straus and Giroux, 1975). Earlier detailed reports on Brazil were published by Amnesty in 1973 and 1974.

[38] Morris's account may be found in his "In the Presence of Mine Enemies," *Harper's Magazine*, October 1975.

[39] Typical of Brazilian worries on this score was a story on "Carter e o Brasil" by Walder de Goes in *Jornal do Brasil*, August 2, 1976.

toward other sources of supply. This has already occurred in jet aircraft. For the truth of the matter is that U.S. aid to Brazil is insignificant economically and marginal militarily. The most obvious targets for liberal and radical critics, such as the USAID Public Safety Program, had already been phased out in 1972. As a result it would be extremely difficult, if not impossible, to show direct U.S. taxpayer participation in police or military torture.

So there is *not* a large U.S. aid program to authoritarian Brazil which might draw the axe of a new administration. Whatever the cuts in budgeting programs, the Pentagon can be expected to maintain its close relations with the Brazilian military, although U.S. officials are clearly concerned that congressional limitations on arms sales may inevitably weaken these ties. These are among the most extensive military relations maintained by the United States with any lesser developed countries. They undoubtedly produce a wealth of information and help to maintain an extraordinarily detailed knowledge of the Brazilian military mentality and governmental predispositions.

The February 21st Memorandum: Reflections and Prospects. How does the U.S.-Brazilian agreement (signed on the occasion of Secretary Kissinger's visit to Brasília on February 21, 1976) fit into this projection?[40] A preliminary analysis suggests the following: (1) initiative for the accord came from the Brazilian Foreign Ministry, which regards it as a direct means to gaining greater attention from policy makers in Washington, especially on economic issues; (2) Washington saw the agreement as "acknowledging a reality"—that is, Brazil's clear emergence as the predominant Latin American power, largely traceable to its rapid economic growth since 1968; (3) since Brazil already had similar consultative understandings with France, the United Kingdom, and West Germany, the Kissinger-Silveira agreement was considered by the Brazilian government to be one more vehicle for avoiding misunderstandings with a major power, but in no sense an "exclusive" obligation; (4) neither Washington nor Brasília seemed concerned over the negative impact this bilateral accord might have on relations with other countries in Latin America, such as Argentina or Venezuela; (5) Brasília and Washington may have very different assumptions about how the accord will affect Brazil's attitude on North-South economic issues. Some U.S. policy makers apparently hope that Brazil will now be less inclined toward an aggressive "Third

---

[40] This section is based in part on interviews with U.S. State Department officials in March 1976 and with officials of the Brazilian Ministry of Foreign Relations in July 1976.

World" strategy in economic matters. Some Brazilians, on the other hand, believe that the agreement may increase their access to, and their leverage on, U.S. government decision makers, *without* prejudicing their continuing economic offensive elsewhere in the world; (6) the memorandum may in part be seen as an instrument being used by both foreign ministers in their continuous bureaucratic struggles to increase control over the process of foreign policy decision making in Brasília and Washington.

At the very least, the memorandum must be regarded as a sign that the current Brazilian government values the U.S. alliance highly enough to join the hemispheric superpower in reaffirming "the solidarity of the Western World" (the phrase in the text), however archaic that might sound to Brazil's erstwhile Third World allies. There are two immediate causes which help to explain Brazil's enthusiastic promotion of the new agreement.

The first cause is Brazil's current balance-of-payments crisis, which has accentuated the country's economic dependence on the United States. In 1975 Brazil suffered a $1.6 billion deficit in trade with the United States, and by the end of the year owed United States commercial banks over $3 billion in relatively short-term debt. As this balance-of-payments crisis continues into 1977, Brazil must protect its credit-worthiness in New York and defend its access to United States markets. Brasília may have seen the reaffirmation of political allegiance in the memorandum as a relatively inexpensive means of enlisting greater bilateral support from Washington on bread-and-butter economic needs.

A second possible cause from the Brazilian side is the revival of cold-war-style anti-Communist apprehensions, especially among the higher military. The Portuguese coup and subsequent radicalization, although apparently arrested by late 1975, frightened many conservative Brazilians, who are especially sensitive to political trends in the former mother country. More than a few Brazilian military officers watched with horror as their Portuguese counterparts lurched toward a Communist-dominated government in 1975. They became equally upset over Soviet, and especially Cuban, intervention in Angola, the former Portuguese colony with strong historic ties to Brazil and a post in what Brazilians call their "Atlantic frontier." To compound their consternation, Brazil proved to be the first major country to recognize the pro-Soviet MPLA. This made Foreign Minister Azeredo da Silveira highly vulnerable to criticism from military officers, many of whom were also disturbed because of President Geisel's removal of Second Army commander d'Avila in January. Thus Silveira's memorandum, which he had been urging on the U.S. government for some time, provided a convenient means for the foreign minister to recoup his position with the President. Geisel was receptive because he knew that his highly anti-Communist military critics (and some civilians, such as those represented by *O Estado de São Paulo*) would be pleased by a reemphasis on the U.S. alliance, which they have regarded as a lodestar of the Revolution of 1964, especially in moments of geopolitical preoccupation such as that provoked by the radicalization of Portugal and Angola.

Finally, what can we conclude about the probable future course of U.S.-Brazilian relations? First, projections here are based on an assumption that the industrial economies will continue their recovery from their worst decline since 1945. If the world economy were to slip back into a new and perhaps even deeper slump, then Brazil would probably take drastic steps to protect its economic interests— as happened in the Great Depression of the 1930s. But in that case Brazil's reaction would be only one—relatively minor—aspect of a worldwide deterioration in economic relations.

Second, we should not dismiss the influence of tradition and expectations in U.S.-Brazilian relations. Aside from the deliberate calculation of interests on both sides, policy makers in Brasília and Washington continue to *believe* in a special relationship between their countries. Obviously that predisposition will not withstand a steady divergence of real interests. U.S. reluctance to supply sophisticated weapons—F-5 fighter planes as a key example—provoked many Brazilian military officers to question the value of the "special relationship." On the other hand, economic dependence has forced Brazil to acknowledge that despite trade and credit diversification, the stakes remain very high in Brazilian connections with the United States. In this mixed picture the weight of tradition plays a role. Despite conflict on specific issues, Brazilian and U.S. policy makers still think that an appeal to "political will" on both sides can pay off in practical terms. The February 21st memorandum is a dramatic reassertion of that mutual predisposition. Only time will tell whether it is anything more than the coincidence of wishful thinking by two foreign ministers under grave pressure on their respective home fronts.

2

THE BRAZILIAN GROWTH AND DEVELOPMENT EXPERIENCE: 1964-1975

Werner Baer

Introduction

Debate over the adequacy of the economic growth pattern of Brazil has been continual through the last twenty-five years, and usually sharpens in times of crises. Stagnation from 1962 to 1967 led to critical examinations of the import substitution industrialization policies of the fifties. One school of thought believed that import substitution industrialization applied to a traditional society without accompanying basic socioeconomic reforms would inevitably lead to stagnation as a result of a limited market. Another group believed that stagnation was the result of distortions from an unbalanced growth process—inflationary finance of infrastructure investments, distortions in relative prices as a result of selective controls, overvalued exchange rates, rigidities in the country's export structure, and so on.[1]

The remarkable expansion of the Brazilian economy in the years 1968–74 did not mute the debate. The defenders of the regime spent their time analyzing the favorable results of the policies of the post-1964 governments, while the critics worried about the distribution of the benefits and the distribution of growth among the sectors. In

---

I wish to thank Donald Coes for many helpful suggestions.
[1] The first group's arguments can be found in such works as: Celso Furtado, *Um Projeto Para O Brasil* (Rio de Janeiro: Editora Saga S.A., 1968), and Maria da Conceição Tavares, *Da substituição de importações ao capitalismo financeiro* (Rio de Janeiro: Zahar Editores, 1972). The second group's thoughts are well represented in such works as Mario H. Simonsen, *Brasil 2001* (Rio de Janeiro: APEC Editora S.A., 1969), and "Brazilian Inflation: Postwar Experience and Outcome of the 1964 Reforms," in *Economic Development Issues: Latin America* (New York: Committee for Economic Development, Supplementary Paper No. 21, August 1967).

fact, the debate during the boom implicitly centered on the question whether Brazil's growth also represented development.[2]

The pronounced decline of Brazil's growth rate in 1975 and the severe balance-of-payments crisis is, once again, centering the debate on the viability of the Brazilian economy as it has evolved in the last ten years. Defenders of the regime attribute the current crisis to external forces—that is, to the world oil crisis and the recession in the industrial countries of the world. Critics of the regime believe that the collapse of the boom was due to some fundamental contradictions within the growth model adopted after the change of regime in 1964.

In this essay I shall analyze the nature of the Brazilian growth experience in the period since 1964 in the hopes of clarifying two questions: to what extent did economic growth over the period produce socioeconomic development? and to what extent is the current crisis the result of short-run external phenomena and to what extent is it linked to so-called "internal contradictions" which evolved over the last decade?

Import Substitution Industrialization

Throughout most of the 1950s Brazilian governments pursued intensive import substitution industrialization programs. These include the erection of high protective tariff walls, various methods of foreign exchange controls, government spending on infrastructure projects and direct investment in a number of industrial enterprises, special inducements to foreign capital, and the establishment of a government development bank.[3] The net result of these efforts was that the Brazilian economy experienced relatively high real growth rates in the period 1950–61—the real gross domestic product (GDP) expanded at yearly growth rates of over 6 percent and industrial production at yearly growth rates of 10 percent. The imbalances and distortions which this intense import substitution industrialization process

---

[2] For the defenders' side see Mario H. Simonsen and Roberto de Oliveira Campos, *A nova economia brasileira* (Rio de Janeiro: Livraria José Olympio Editora, 1974). On the critics' side, see Celso Furtado, *O mito do desenvolvimento econômico* (Rio de Janeiro: Editora Paz e Terra S.A., 1974), and Ricardo Tolipan and Arthur Carlos Tirelli, eds., *A controvérsia sobre distribuição de renda e desenvolvimento* (Rio de Janeiro: Zahar Editores, 1975).

[3] For details see Werner Baer, *Industrialization and Economic Development in Brazil* (Homewood, Illinois: Richard D. Irwin, Inc., 1965), chs. 3-5, and Joel Bergsman, *Brazil: Industrialization and Trade Policies* (New York and London: Oxford University Press, 1970), chs. 3 and 4.

brought along have been well documented in the literature.[4] The industrialization accentuated the unequal regional distribution of Brazil's income—most of the new industries were located in the Center-South region (mostly in the São Paulo-Rio-Belo Horizonte area); few investment resources were applied to the modernization of agriculture; the capital-intensive nature of the new industries contributed toward increasing the concentration in the income distribution; the combination of inflationary finance and selected price controls produced distortions in the allocation of resources; and over the years the country's balance of payments became increasingly strained as a result of substantial lags in adjusting the exchange rate while the domestic price level was rising, as well as of continued reliance on traditional exports whose prices in the world market were weakening.

With the fading of the import substitution industrialization boom at the beginning of the 1960s, the Brazilian economy entered a seven-year period of stagnation, during which the real GDP grew at yearly rates of 3.7 percent. It has never been fully established to what extent the decline in the growth rate after 1961 was due to the political instability Brazil experienced in the early 1960s, to what extent to the imbalances and distortions that had accumulated over the preceding decade, and to what extent to the failure of domestic or foreign markets to expand and replace the dynamism of import substitution industrialization.[5]

Post-1964 Policies and Achievements

The economists who shaped Brazil's policies after the 1964 change of regime belonged to the school of thought that attributed the decline of the economy's dynamism to the imbalanced way in which it had grown during the import substitution industrialization years, and to the distortions in the allocation of resources that had resulted from the combination of inflation and price controls.

[4] Baer, *Industrialization and Economic Development in Brazil*, ch. 7; Werner Baer and Mario H. Simonsen, "Profit Illusion and Policy-Making in an Inflationary Economy," in *Oxford Economic Papers* (July 1965); Donald E. Syvrud, *Foundations of Brazilian Economic Growth*, AEI-Hoover Research Publications 1 (Stanford, California: Hoover Institution Press, 1974), chs. 2, 4, 5, 9; Stefan H. Robock, *Brazil: A Study in Development Progress* (Lexington, Massachusetts: Lexington Books, D. C. Heath and Company, 1975).

[5] Werner Baer and Isaac Kerstenetzky, "The Brazilian Economy," in Riordan Roett, ed., *Brazil in the Sixties* (Nashville, Tennessee: Vanderbilt University Press, 1972), and Syvrud, *Foundations of Brazilian Economic Growth*, ch. 2.

Post-1964 Policies. The immediate concerns of the policy makers were control of inflation (which by the mid-1960s had reached yearly rates of over 100 percent), elimination of distortions in the price structure and in the allocation of resources. Classic stabilization policies were adopted—curtailing government expenditures in a number of sectors, increasing tax revenues as a result of improvements in the tax-collection system, tightening credit, and squeezing the wage sector.[6] Measures were also adopted to eliminate price distortions. For instance, public utility rates (which are government controlled and which had lagged behind the general price increase) were raised drastically. Although this had an additional short-run inflationary impact (this being what is known as "corrective inflation"), such measures led to the gradual elimination of deficits in various sectors (for example, transportation), reducing the necessity for government subsidies, and thus contributing to the decline of government budget deficits.

These policy actions resulted in a steady decline in the government's budget deficit. In 1963 the deficit amounted to 4.3 percent of the GDP; by 1971 this proportion had declined to 0.3 percent. The inflation rate was brought down gradually to about 20 percent, where it hovered in the boom years 1968–74.

The modernization and strengthening of capital markets was also deemed essential for sustained economic growth. The indexing of financial instruments was instituted—that is, a system was set up whereby the principal and interest on debt instruments were readjusted in accordance with the rate of inflation.[7] It was initially applied to government bonds, making it possible for the government to rely increasingly on noninflationary financing of the budget deficit. Over the years it was extended to other financial instruments. For example, the newly created housing bank (BNH) was allowed to issue indexed bonds and to index its loans. Indexing was extended to savings deposits, savings and loan associations and corporate debts, and a mechanism was developed for periodic revaluation of the capital of firms in accordance with price changes.

A capital market law, instituted in 1965, provided an institutional setting for strengthening and increasing the use of the stock market

---

[6] For details of policies in the mid 1960s see Baer and Kerstenetzky, "The Brazilian Economy," and Werner Baer, "The Brazilian Boom, 1968-72: An Explanation and Interpretation," *World Development*, vol. 1, no. 8 (August 1973).

[7] Werner Baer and Paul Beckerman, "Indexing in Brazil," *World Development*, vol. 2, no. 12 (December 1974); Albert Fishlow, "Indexing Brazilian Style: Inflation Without Tears," *Brookings Papers on Economic Activity*, 1974:1 (Washington, D.C.: Brookings Institution, 1974).

and encouraged the establishment of investment banks to underwrite new issues. New credit mechanisms were gradually developed to increase the demand of investors and consumers for the output of Brazil's growing industrial capacity. Many special funds were created, functioning as adjuncts of the government development bank (BNDE), to finance (for example) the sales of small and medium-size Brazilian firms or finance the acquisition of capital goods.[8]

A large proportion of the resources for these official credit institutions was provided by a system of forced savings whose burden was borne to a large extent by the working classes. Since the late 1960s a number of social security and retirement funds have provided an increasing proportion of national savings, comprising the bulk of the funds borrowed by the national treasury, the housing bank, and resources used by the BNDE and the official savings banks (Caixas Econômicas). These savings, of course, were all indexed.[9]

Over the decade 1964–74 the Brazilian government made increasing use of tax incentives to influence the allocation of resources among regions and sectors. For instance, heavy use was made of an already existing tax-incentive mechanism connected with SUDENE (the development agency for the Northeast region of Brazil) to attract investors to that backward region; the mechanism was subsequently extended to the Amazon area. Among other tax measures were incentives to stimulate export, tourism, reforestation, and the stock market.[10]

Government investment expenditures were never cut back during the vigorous stabilization years after 1964, as existing infrastructure projects were continued. Also, while the financial reforms and stabilization programs mentioned above were being carried out, the government engaged in some basic sectoral studies (in collaboration with the U.S. Agency for International Development, the World Bank, and the Inter-American Development Bank) designed to guide the expansion of the country's power supply, transportation system, urban infrastructure, and heavy industries—especially steel, mining, and petrochemicals—which were dominated by government enterprises. The time-lag between these studies, negotiations to finance investment, and actual investment activities, came to three or four years

[8] For greater details, see Simonsen and Campos, *A nova economia brasileira*, ch. 6; Walter L. Ness, Jr., "Financial Markets Innovation as a Development Strategy: Initial Results from the Brazilian Experience," *Economic Development and Cultural Change*, vol. 22, no. 8 (April 1974).

[9] For a thorough description of how these funds are organized, see Julian Chacel, Mario H. Simonsen, and Arnoldo Wald, *A correção monetária* (Rio de Janeiro: APEC Editora S.A., 1970).

[10] Simonsen and Campos, *A nova economia brasileira*, pp. 137-150.

and only in the late 1960s were the results of such planning activities felt.[11]

Finally, foreign economic trade policy was considered of central importance by post-1964 governments. The rapid growth and diversification of exports was deemed essential to the recovery and long-term health of the Brazilian economy. To achieve these goals the government adopted a number of policies over the years, including the abolition of state export taxes, simplification of administrative procedures for exporters, and the introduction of tax incentives and subsidized credit. At least as important was the adoption in 1968 of a more realistic exchange rate policy, consisting of frequent (but unpredictable) small devaluations of the cruzeiro. It was hoped that in this way the cruzeiro could be kept from becoming overvalued as inflation continued, while keeping speculation against the currency at a minimum and keeping the exchange rate from becoming a political issue.

Achievements of the Post-1964 Governments. The stagnation evident in the Brazilian economy by 1962 continued after the change of regime in 1964 and lasted until 1968. It can be attributed to a combination of factors: the effects of the stabilization measures applied in those years; the time-lag involved before the effects of the institutional reforms in the financial system could be felt and before the numerous studies and plans for the expansion of the country's infrastructure and heavy industries could result in actual construction activities; and, finally, the time-lag involved in convincing the domestic and foreign private and official investors of the new regime's stability and control over the economy.

The Brazilian economy entered its remarkable seven-year boom in 1968. Annual real growth of the GDP, which averaged only 3.7 percent in the period 1962–67, surged to yearly rates averaging 10.1 percent in the years 1968–74. As will be noted from Table 1, industry was the leading sector, expanding at yearly rates of 12.2 percent. Within manufacturing, one observes (Table 2) that the highest growth rates were achieved by such sectors as transport equipment, machinery, and electrical equipment, while traditional sectors like textiles, clothing, and food products experienced much slower rates of growth. In other words, much of the manufacturing growth was concentrated in consumer durables and chemicals. The expansion of the Brazilian economy can be illustrated more graphically by men-

---

[11] Greater details can be found in Werner Baer, "The Brazilian Boom, 1968-72," and Syvrud, *Foundations of Brazilian Economic Growth*, ch. 6.

Table 1
YEARLY GROWTH RATES OF REAL GDP, PER CAPITA GDP, INDUSTRY AND AGRICULTURE
(percent)

Years	Real GDP	Per Capita Real GDP	Industry	Agriculture
1956–62 [a]	7.8	4.0	10.3	5.7
1962–67 [a]	3.7	1.3	3.9	4.0
1968	9.3	6.3	15.0	1.5
1969	9.0	5.9	11.0	6.0
1970	9.5	6.4	11.1	5.6
1971	11.3	8.2	11.2	12.2
1972	10.4	7.3	13.8	4.1
1973	11.4	8.3	15.0	3.5
1974	9.6	6.5	8.2	8.5
1975	4.0	1.3	4.2	3.4

[a] Yearly average.
Source: Calculated from data of Centro de Contas Nacionais, Fundação Getúlio Vargas. Published in *Conjuntura Econômica* (various issues).

tion of a few numbers of actual output in both basic industries and consumer goods industries: Steel output grew from 2.8 million tons in 1964 to 8.3 million in 1975; installed electric power capacity expanded from 6,840,000 megawatts to 19,500,500 in the same period; cement from 5.6 to 17.9 million tons; motor vehicles from 184,000 to 930,000, and passenger cars from 98,000 to 524,000; paper from 0.6 to 1.6 million tons; by 1974, television set production had reached 831,000 and production of refrigerators 658,000. The average yearly growth rate of road construction increased from 12 percent in the period 1964–67 to 25 percent in 1968–72 and the rate of growth of paving from 6 percent to 33 percent.[12]

Tables 3, 4, and 5 summarize Brazil's foreign trade position. External trade grew at rates substantially higher than the growth of the economy as a whole. In the years 1970–73 the average yearly growth rate of exports was 14.7 percent and of imports 21 percent. The trade deficit resulting from the higher import growth was in-

---

[12] These data were obtained from the annual publication of Instituto Brasileiro de Geografia e Estatística, *Anuário Estatístico do Brasil*.

Table 2
AVERAGE ANNUAL GROWTH RATES OF
INDIVIDUAL SECTORS
(percent)

	1967–70	1971	1972	1973	1974
Nonmetal minerals	17.3	11.1	13.7	16.4	15.1
Metal products	14.4	5.6	12.1	6.3	4.3
Machinery	22.7	3.6	} 18.9	} 27.8	} 11.6
Electrical equipment	13.4	21.3			
Transport equipment	32.6	19.0	22.5	27.6	19.1
Paper and paper products	9.1	6.3	7.0	10.1	3.5
Rubber products	15.3	11.8	13.0	12.4	10.8
Chemicals	15.6	13.6	16.3	22.3	8.5
Textiles	7.4	8.8	} 4.1	} 8.4	} −2.8
Clothing, shoes, etc.	1.7	−1.8			
Food products	8.3	3.6	} 13.3	} 9.6	} 4.4
Beverages	8.2	4.8			
Tobacco	9.6	5.7			
Total Manufacturing	14.2	11.6	13.6	15.8	7.1
Construction	14.4	8.4	13.0	15.4[a]	11.2[a]
Public utilities	12.2	N.A.	11.1	12.5[a]	12.0[a]

[a] Estimates based on January-November results in 1973 and 1974.

N.A. = not available.

Source: Same as Table 1.

creased still further by a rising deficit in the service balance. Until 1974, however, this was more than covered by a massive inflow of official and private capital. The net inflow of direct investment grew from a yearly average of US$ 84 million in the period of 1965–69 to $977 and $944 million in the years 1973 and 1974, respectively. Even more notable were net foreign loans, which increased from a yearly average of $604 million in 1965–69 to $4.5 and $6.6 billion in 1973 and 1974. Foreign financing substantially exceeded the deficit of the current account, resulting in an increase in Brazil's foreign exchange reserves from an average of $400 million in the period 1965–69 to $6.8 billion in 1973.

It should also be noted (in Table 5) that in these years Brazil succeeded in diversifying its commodity export structure. The portion of the value of exports accounted for by coffee declined from an

Table 3

BRAZIL'S FOREIGN ECONOMIC POSITION: BALANCE OF PAYMENTS POSITION
(U.S. $ billions)

	1960–64ᵃ	1965–69ᵃ	1969	1970	1971	1972	1973	1974	1975
Exports	1.34	1.84	2.31	2.74	2.90	3.99	6.20	7.95	8.66
Imports	1.25	1.51	1.99	2.51	3.25	4.23	6.19	12.63	12.17
Trade balance	.91	.33	.32	.23	−.35	−.24	.01	−4.68	−3.51
Service balance	−.34	−.51	−.64	−.82	−.98	−1.25	−1.72	−2.31	−3.56
Net foreign direct investment	.07	.08	.14	.12	.17	.38	.98	.94	.97
Net foreign loans	.35	.61	1.05	1.44	2.52	4.30	4.30	7.37	4.90
Foreign debt	2.90	—	4.40	5.30	6.60	10.20	12.60	17.40	22.00
Reserves	—	.40	.65	1.19	1.72	3.90	6.80	5.70	4.00

ᵃ Yearly average.
Source: *Boletim do Banco Central do Brasil.*

Table 4
BRAZIL'S EXPORT AND IMPORT COEFFICIENTS
(percent)

	1950	1961	1964	1970	1971	1972	1973	1974
Export/GDP	9.2	6.0	5.1	5.0	6.0	7.0	8.0	8.0
Import/GDP	7.4	7.4	5.4	6.0	7.0	8.0	9.0	14.0

Source: Calculated from Instituto Brasileiro de Geografia e Estatística, *Anuário Estatístico* (Brasília, various dates).

Table 5
EXPORT COMMODITY STRUCTURE
(percent)

	1965–69	1968–72	1973	1974
Coffee	42.0	32.6	21.7	12.6
Iron ore	6.1	6.7	5.9	7.2
Soybeans	—	1.6	8.0	7.4
Sugar	5.0	6.5	8.9	15.8
Meat	1.9	3.3	3.1	0.9
Manufactures	7.2	15.8	22.0	27.7
Other	37.8	33.5	30.4	28.4
Total	100.0	100.0	100.0	100.0

Source: Calculated from Instituto Brasileiro de Geografia e Estatística, *Anuário Estatístico* (Brasília, various dates).

average of 42 percent in the mid-1960s to 12.6 percent in 1974; sugar rose from 5.0 percent in 1965–69 to 15.8 percent in 1974; manufactures increased from 7.2 to 27.7 percent in the 1965–74 period; soybeans were not a part of Brazil's export structure in the mid-1960s and stood at 7.4 percent in 1974. The import commodity structure was noted for the growth of capital goods, whose portion of total imports rose from about 31 percent in the mid-1960s to about 40 percent in the mid-1970s. And with the world oil crisis, petroleum imports rose from 11.5 percent of imports in 1973 to about 25 percent in 1975.

The post-1964 policies clearly opened the economy to foreign trade. Whereas the import substitution policies of the 1950s decreased the foreign trade coefficients (that is, resulted in a decline in the export/GDP and import/GDP ratios), the opposite result occurred as a result of the post-1964 policies, especially in the early 1970s (see Table 4).

The Government Sector. One aspect of Brazil's economic growth which is only beginning to receive attention is the large and growing involvement of the state in Brazil's economy.[13] Government expenditures (all levels of government) as a proportion of GDP have grown from 17.1 percent in 1947 to 37.0 percent in 1973. State enterprises dominate in steel, mining, and petrochemicals. They control over 80 percent of power-generating capacity and most of the public utilities. It has been estimated that in 1974, for the 100 largest firms (in value of assets), 74 percent of the combined assets belonged to state enterprises; while, for the 5,113 largest firms, only half as much— 37 percent—of the assets belonged to state enterprises.[14] Similarly, state banks play a dominant role in the financial system. Of the fifty largest banks (in deposits), state banks accounted for about 56 percent of total deposits in 1974 and about 65 percent of loans to the private sector.[15]

I have suggested elsewhere that much of the growth since 1968 is due to the impact of government programs,[16] and that, given the elaborate control mechanisms of the state, the allocation of resources is more the result of government policies than of market forces. Much work remains to be done, however, to understand the relationships among the "tripé" of the Brazilian economy—that is, the private domestic sector, the multinational-dominated sectors, and the government sector. Who influences whom? Which sector takes the initiative?

Issues Surrounding the Brazilian Growth Experience, 1964–74

The Equity Question. It has been generally recognized that the fruits of the rapid expansion of the Brazilian economy have been unevenly distributed. This became apparent with the publication of the 1970 demographic census which revealed an increase in the concentration of the distribution of income. As can be seen from Table 6, the share

---

[13] Werner Baer, Isaac Kerstenetzky, and Annibal V. Villela, "The Changing Role of the State in the Brazilian Economy," *World Development*, vol. 1, no. 11 (November 1973).

[14] "Quem é Quem Na Economia Brasileira," *Visão*, August 31, 1975, p. 27.

[15] Ibid., p. 573.

[16] Werner Baer, "The Brazilian Boom, 1968-72."

Table 6
CHANGES IN BRAZIL'S INCOME DISTRIBUTION

	1960	1970	Per Capita Income in U.S. Dollars	
			1960	1970
Lower 40%	11.2	9.0	84	90
Next 40%	34.3	27.8	257	278
Next 15%	27.0	27.0	540	720
Top 5%	27.4	36.3	1,645	2,940
Total	100.0	100.0 (Average)	300	400

Source: Calculated from IBGE, *Censo Demográfico*, 1970.

of the national income of the lowest 40 percent of the income recipients declined from 11.2 percent in 1960 to 9 percent in 1970; the share of the next 40 percent fell from 34.4 to 27.8 percent, while the top 5 percent increased their share from 27.4 to 36.3 percent. There is also considerable evidence that real wages declined at first in the second half of the 1960s and then rose at a rate substantially smaller than the rate of productivity increases.[17]

Although Table 7 shows minimum rather than average wages, one should take it into account that, in the states of Rio de Janeiro and São Paulo, over 25 percent of the 1973 work force in manufacturing earned one minimum salary or less and over 30 percent of workers in commerce earned one minimum salary or less, while workers earning two minimum salaries or less amounted to 65 and 70 percent in the respective sectors; the situation was much worse in the Northeast.[18] Sample surveys in 1972 revealed that fewer than 40 percent of Brazil's urban households had access to a general water supply system, fewer than 43 percent were connected with a general sewage system or had septic tanks, only 53 percent had electricity, and only 5 percent had telephones. Moreover, there were huge variations among regions.[19]

---

[17] John Wells, "Distribution of Earnings, Growth and the Structure of Demand in Brazil during the Sixties," *World Development*, vol. 2, no. 1 (January 1974), p. 10.

[18] These numbers were calculated from data in Programa Nacional de Amostragem de Domicílios (PNAD), *População, Mão de Obra, Salário, Instrução, Domicílio*, 4th trimester 1973. The minimum salary, decreed by the government, is that salary which enterprises must pay their workers—like the U.S. minimum wage.

[19] Data calculated from PNAD survey, IBGE, 1972.

Table 7

MINIMUM WAGES IN CONSTANT 1965 PRICES

(Cr$ per month)

	1966	1967	1968	1969	1970	1971	1972	1973	1974	1975 [a]
Rio de Janeiro	53.9	53.1	52.9	51.2	50.8	51.9	54.2	55.3	49.9	56.2
São Paulo	50.9	50.8	50.0	49.1	50.2	50.2	50.9	51.8	47.1	53.1
Porto Alegre	49.2	50.4	51.2	51.5	50.6	51.7	52.3	49.9	47.1	51.4

[a] All numbers refer to December of each year; 1975 to October.

Source: *Boletim do Banco Central do Brasil*, December 1975, p. 127.

The first question that is raised by this distributional situation is whether the situation will ultimately lead to stagnation, inasmuch as the small proportion of the population (see Table 6) will not constitute a large enough market to sustain a high rate of economic growth. But for two reasons the stagnation argument might not apply to Brazil. First, there is the size of the government sector that if correctly managed, can keep growth going. Second, there is the absolute size of Brazil's population. Even if 20 percent of the population receives over 63 percent of the country's income, this represents about twenty-two million people, which is a large market. It remains to be seen, however, how economic growth could expand rapidly beyond the import substitution industrialization period. This, however, raises another question. Has a new dualism emerged in Brazil, in which two socioeconomic groups will perpetuate themselves side-by-side? This has been described by some as the "Belgium in India" situation—that is, a population of about twenty-two million with a per capita income of about US $1,000 while eighty-five million receive incomes below U.S. $300. Is this dualism permanent? Or assuming no drastic income redistribution policies by decree, would the dynamism inherent in a market serving twenty-two million people gradually draw an increasingly larger number of the eighty-five million into the higher income society? [20]

Even though the increasingly unequal distribution of income might not lead to long-term stagnation, the issue has been central to the debate between the defenders and the critics of the regime. The basic reason for its centrality was that a system producing high rates of growth of a product distributed in a blatantly unequal fashion seemed in the long run to be both morally and politically unjustifiable. The defenders of the regime argued, however, that the very success of the Brazilian growth experience of the late 1960s and early 1970s had produced an increase in the concentration of income, because the high growth rates increased the demand for skilled manpower, which was in short supply. Market forces thus caused an immense rise in the relative income of skilled laborers, technicians and managers, which meant that a large proportion of the increment in the real income was captured by groups with large amounts of scarce human capital.[21]

[20] For more formal analyses of an emerging dualist society, see E. Bacha and L. Taylor, "Unequalizing Spiral: A First Growth Model for Belindia," Discussion Paper No. 15, Department of Economics, University of Brasília, 1973; E. Bacha, "Distribution and Growth in Belindia: A Structuralist Synthesis," Discussion Paper No. 17, Department of Economics, University of Brasília, 1974.
[21] Carlos Geraldo Langoni, *Distribuição de renda e desenvolvimento econômico*

In the view of these defenders the solution to the problem lies in increased investment in education, which would gradually improve the country's income distribution by raising the supply of skilled labor relative to demand and thus causing a decrease in the difference between the remuneration for different kinds of labor.[22] Simonsen and Campos believe that the government has chosen the most adequate way for reconciling maximum growth with an improvement in the distribution of income. The improvement in distribution is being achieved in an indirect manner "through an extension of free education, an improvement in the educational pyramid, credit facilities for low income housing, small businesses and small rural establishments, retirement benefits for rural workers and the creation of the retirement funds for industrial and government workers and the program for social integration." [23]

Critics have viewed this kind of analysis as being incomplete at best and as an apology for the policies of post-1964 governments at worst. If the basic explanation of the rise in the concentration of income in the 1960s were related to the scarcity of skilled labor, of course little direct blame could be placed on the specific government policies since 1964. But many of the critics have argued that in fact the "education" explanation was of minor importance, and a number have blamed the increase in the concentration of income on the wage policies which were instituted after 1964.[24] There is substantial evidence that real minimum wages and average industrial wages declined during the stabilization years. John Wells has shown that even after real wages began to rise again in the late 1960s, they lagged substantially behind productivity increases, thus contributing to continuing deterioration in the distribution of income beweeen labor and capital.[25]

Other elements contributing to the income concentration have been cited by various critics, and one of them is technology. Over time Brazil's industries have become increasingly capital-intensive. Thus, with industry as the leading sector—having a capital/labor

---

do Brasil (Rio de Janeiro: Editora Expressão e Cultura, 1973), ch. 5; Simonsen and Campos, *A nova economia brasileira*, pp. 185-187.

[22] Langoni, *Distribuição da renda*, ch. 19.

[23] Simonsen and Campos, *A nova economia brasileira*, p. 187.

[24] Tolipan and Tinelli, *A controvérsia sobre distribuição*, especially articles by A. Fishlow and Rodolfo Hoffman; E. Bacha, "Recent Brazilian Economic Growth and some of Its Main Problems," Discussion Paper No. 25, Department of Economics, University of Brasília, April 1975.

[25] Wells, "Distribution of Earnings, Growth and the Structure of Demand in Brazil during the Sixties."

ratio that is much higher than the ratio in the traditional sectors—increased concentration in the distribution of income is bound to occur, all other things being equal.[26] This will be the case even though labor in the capital-intensive industries receives higher real wages than in other sectors, inasmuch as total labor used is small relative to capital and other nonlabor inputs. A second factor, beside technology, was the widespread use of tax incentives to allocate resources, which has inevitably favored the higher income groups. These groups were in a position to make use of the incentives, contributing to the increased concentration in income.[27]

Who Saves? One traditional justification for a concentration in the distribution of income has been that the upper income groups have a greater propensity to save than the lower income groups. Thus, to increase investment and future productive capacity, income concentration must be tolerated for a while. Simonsen and Campos, for instance, have stated that "the so-called 'Brazilian Miracle' must be credited to the sacrifices which were endured during the Castello Branco administration. [It was rooted in the] orthodox recognition that any type of developmental process has to be based on savings and market considerations: the first requirement for rapid and sustained growth is a high rate of savings." [28]

Brazilian savings have experienced a remarkable growth since the late 1950s and early 1960s. Revised national accounts data show that domestic savings as a proportion of GDP stood at 17.5 percent in 1959; by 1973 the figure had risen to 21 percent. According to these data, however, most of the increment in savings came from the government sector—the government saving/GDP ratio having risen from 5.1 percent in 1959 to 8.4 percent in 1973.[29]

An estimate shows the sum of the various social program funds representing forced savings (the unemployment fund FGTS, PIS, and PASEP, which did not exist in 1959) at 14 percent of total savings for 1973. With government savings for that year they account for 52 percent of total savings. Preliminary estimates for 1974 show that the rapid growth of the unemployment and retirement funds con-

---

[26] Hoffman in Tolipan and Tinelli, *A controvérsia sobre distribuição*, p. 11, and Baer, "The Brazilian Boom, 1968-72," p. 6.

[27] Fishlow in Tolipan and Tinelli, *A controvérsia sobre distribuição*, p. 185, and Baer, "The Brazilian Boom, 1968-72," pp. 6-7.

[28] Simonsen and Campos, *A nova economia brasileira*, p. 10.

[29] Data from Fundação Getúlio Vargas, Centro de Contas Nacionais, *Sistema de Contas Nacionais, Nova Estimativas* (Rio de Janeiro, September 1974).

tinued, with their proportion of total savings rising from 14 percent in 1973 to 17 percent in 1974.

These data lead to some skepticism about the alleged link between the distribution of income and the economy's savings behavior. In addition, the rapid rise of consumer durable consumption of the more favored income groups would seem to indicate that the system (that is, consumer credit and the availability of an increasing variety of consumer goods) encourages them to consume rather than to save.[30] A recent study suggests that a large portion of the indexed credit of the housing bank, whose funds are drawn from the retirement funds mentioned above, have been used to finance middle and upper income housing, other urban construction, and urban infrastructure, rather than housing for the poor.[31] This would be an additional instance of forced savings by lower income groups financing projects for the more favored income classes.

Demand and Production Profiles. Increased concentration of income raises a further problem, rarely discussed until recently: increased investment in a society with concentrated incomes produces a production capacity profile which is unlikely to be adequate for a more egalitarian society. This problem is closely related to the arguments developed by Furtado in his recent critiques of the Brazilian model. He argues that the profile of the productive structure that has evolved in Brazil over the last decades mirrors the demand profile of the population, which in turn, is influenced by the distribution of income.

> The concentration in the distribution of income of Brazil resulted in a demand profile in which the goods of technologically advanced industries are heavily represented. This is also reflected in the country's productive structure. Thus, the continued dynamism of technologically advanced industries depends on the maintenance or even on an increase in the concentration of income.[32]

The tax incentive programs, the emergent financial structure characterized by increasing amounts of credit institutions catering to the financing of consumer durables, and the growth of an absolutely

---

[30] Wells came to the same conclusion after examining the few consumer budget surveys available. See Wells, "Distribution of Earnings, Growth and the Structure of Demand in Brazil during the Sixties," pp. 20-24.

[31] Clark W. Reynolds and Robert T. Carpenter, "Housing Finance in Brazil: Toward a New Distribution of Wealth," in Wayne A. Cornelius and Felicity M. Trueblood, eds., *Latin American Urban Research*, vol. 5 (Beverly Hills: SAGE Publications, 1975), pp. 147-174.

[32] Celso Furtado, *O mito do desenvolvimento econômico* (Rio de Janeiro: Editora Paz e Terra S.A., 1974).

large (though proportionally small) class of managers and skilled laborers with high incomes, has been crucial to maintain the "correct" demand profile.

It has also been suggested (without further elaboration) that the large presence of multinational firms and the sophistication of the financial system have contributed to influence the consumption pattern of the population. Through advertising by the multinationals and through developments in the credit mechanism, new demand has been created for many consumer durables. Some economists have claimed that this has "distorted" the demand profile of the lower income groups, inducing them to buy goods they would normally not purchase, given their income level.[33]

Most of these arguments remain to be tested empirically. Of course, the much faster growth of output in consumer durable industries than in the traditional industries (see Table 2) gives some support to Furtado's analysis. It would be interesting to test the degree of rigidity of the production capacity profile when changes occur in the demand profile. The more rigid it is, the weaker becomes the defense of a temporary increase in the concentration of income, while the more flexible it is, the stronger is the defense.

A large proportion of Brazil's capital formation in the late 1960s and the first half of the 1970s consisted of public investments and investment activities of government enterprises (in 1969 this amounted to as much as 60 percent of total capital formation). The productive profile resulting from these investments does not necessarily imply the need for a demand profile weighted in favor of a minority of wealthier people—increased steel production capacity, petrochemicals, iron ore mining, power generating capacity, urban rapid transit systems, and so on, would all be necessary regardless of the income distribution. One may, however, question the wisdom of the huge government investments in road building, which supported the capacity expansion of the automobile industry and made the country increasingly dependent on the consumption of petroleum, 80 percent of which was imported.

Other Distributional Problems. Although the post-1964 governments have attempted to come to grips with Brazil's age-old problem of regional imbalances, they have made few inroads into the dramatic maldistribution between the Southeast/South and the Northeast. It was mentioned above that this problem was dealt with mainly through

[33] Ibid., Maria de Conceição Tavares, *Da substituição de importações ao capitalismo financiero* (Rio de Janeiro: Zahar Editores, 1972).

the well-known tax incentive program of SUDENE. This resulted in some notable industrial growth in the Northeast, but most of that growth was concentrated in the cities of Salvador and Recife, and most industries were so capital-intensive that they provided few employment opportunities.[34] By 1970, although the Northeast still contained 30.3 percent of the population, it accounted for only 12.2 percent of the national income and only 5.6 percent of industrial output; the Southeast, however, with 42.7 percent of the population, accounted for 64.5 percent of the national income and 80.6 percent of industrial output.[35] The 1972 sample survey of PNAD, moreover, revealed dramatic regional differences in social well-being. In São Paulo, for instance, 85 percent of the households had electricity, while in the Northeast this proportion stood at only 25 percent; 73 percent of the São Paulo households were linked to a sewage system or had septic tanks, but only 15 percent of Northeastern households had this convenience.[36]

The most publicized attempt at a new regional policy was the Transamazon highway project announced by President Médici in September 1970. Huge sums were poured into this project designed for simultaneous road construction and colonization. In addition to the policy makers' desire to increase the population of a huge empty territory—a territory assuming increasing strategic importance in the eyes of Brazil's military—it was also hoped that a massive migration of population would be a relatively efficient way of resolving the socioeconomic problems of such areas as the Northeast. Unfortunately, the Transamazon project was carried out without adequate preliminary planning so that it created more problems than it solved, and by the mid-1970s the project seemed to have fallen to a very low priority in the government's economic policies.

Departure from Post-1964 Orthodoxy

Many of the rules and institutions established by the first post-1964 government helped to produce the high growth rates in the 1968–74 period without the distortions that occurred during the import substitution industrialization boom of the 1950s. It is of interest to note

[34] David E. Goodman and Roberto Cavalcanti de Alburquerque, *Incentivos a industrialização e desenvolvimento do nordeste* (Rio de Janeiro: IPEA, Coleção Relatórios de Pesquisa, No. 20, 1974).

[35] Werner Baer and Pedro Pinchas Geiger, "Industrialization, Urbanization and the Persistence of Regional Inequalities in Brazil" (Instituto Brasileiro de Geografia e Estatística Research Document, January 1976).

[36] Data calculated from Instituto Brasileiro de Geografia e Estatística, PNAD sample surveys, 1972.

how the successor governments, especially in the 1970s, have begun to deviate from some of these rules as a result of internally generated pressure.

One example is the indexing system. The post-1964 governments had enough force to keep the wage sector out of indexing. Also, from the beginning, the agricultural sector was exempt: loans to agriculture always carried an interest rate substantially below the rate of inflation. Loans for agricultural inputs, for instance, cost only 7 percent at a time when inflation was running at three times that rate. This has amounted to a deliberate subsidy to the agricultural sector (the credit most often going to the more privileged farming units).

Subsidization by index exemption has grown in the 1970s. As the many debtors to the housing bank could not keep up their real payments (probably as a result of the lag in money wage increases and the faster increase of the prices of goods other than rent) there was danger of widespread default. The government consequently had to find ways to ease the debt burden through such means as lengthening repayment periods and even lowering the interest rate.

Pressure for exemption from indexing also came from the industrial sector. The public criticisms voiced in 1974–75 against the growth of government and multinational enterprises to the detriment of the Brazilian private sector resulted in the reduction of the monetary correction burden of loans by the government development bank. This amounted, in effect, to massive subsidy through indexation exemption.

These increased exemptions from indexation of borrowing groups have raised uneasy questions about their effects on creditor groups. A large portion of the creditor groups are composed of workers whose savings are invested in pension and social security funds. Should these workers be the ones to subsidize the borrowers or should the burden be borne by the taxpayers in general? According to a policy decision made in 1975, it would seem that the creditors would bear much of the burden. Evidence for this view was provided by the introduction of a new price index for the purpose of indexing: the index is "cleansed" of "accidental phenomena"—such as droughts—on the price level (in Portuguese this has been called the *indice de preços expurgados*). Naturally, the increase of this index has been much slower than the increase in the regular cost-of-living index.[37]

Another violation of the post-1964 rules came in the way the exchange rate policy instituted in 1968 was used in the mid-1970s.

---

[37] For a description of the new index see *Conjuntura Econômica*, November 1975, p. 101.

As the mini-devaluations proceeded, the total yearly devaluations amounted to less than the total rate of inflation minus the inflation of Brazil's trading partners. The resulting overvaluation of the cruzeiro did not matter, however, inasmuch as export incentives (tax incentives and subsidized credits) more than compensated for the overvaluation. By the mid-1970s, however, the total yearly devaluations of the cruzeiro had fallen behind the rate of inflation to such an extent that the competitiveness of Brazil's exports might be affected.

The pressures against devaluation came from two sources. First, there was concern about resurging inflationary forces rekindled by the world oil crisis: too much devaluation was seen as an added source of inflation. Second, during the boom years many Brazilian firms had obtained large amounts of credit from foreign banks: rapid devaluation of the cruzeiro would substantially increase the cost of the debt in cruzeiro terms and thus increase the financial burden on sectors the government has relied upon to continue high levels of investment and production activities.

These two examples indicate that although the Brazilian government has the power to enforce economic decisions on the distribution of resources in accordance with rules originally developed in the mid-1960s, it has found it increasingly difficult to live within those rules as it has been subjected to market pressures beyond its control.

The Oil Crisis and Its Implications

In 1975 Brazil's growth rate declined sharply. Real GDP grew at about 4 percent and the balance-of-payments crisis raised the possibility that the country's growth rate might remain at a low level for the foreseeable future. The world oil crisis and Brazil's investment plans have resulted in rapid growth of imports (the great rise of the import bill was partially caused by increased oil prices and partially by the need to import sophisticated capital goods), which has not been sufficiently offset by export increases. The rise in the current account deficit has necessitated massive borrowings abroad, resulting in an expansion of the foreign debt from $10 billion in 1972 to over $22 billion by the end of 1975. The drastic curtailment of imports, only a fraction of which were finished consumer goods, has contributed to a decline in investment activities and hence in the growth rate.

The immediate reaction of the government has been to promote an accelerated program of import substitution in such industries as heavy capital goods, steel, non-metallic minerals, and fertilizers. One problem, of course, is that in the short run this implies increased imports of capital goods to build such industries; unless substantial foreign financing can be obtained for such projects (which is increasingly more difficult and more expensive with the country's huge indebtedness), such import substitution will have to be achieved in gradual steps.

The Brazilian government has substantially increased the relative price of petroleum. This action, however, did not much curtail the growth in the quantity of petroleum imports. The dilemma the Brazilian policy makers are facing lies in the fact that one of the mainstays of Brazil's industrial growth has been the automobile industry: with the vertical industrial integration process, hundreds of supplying firms have appeared over the last two decades serving the automobile market. Moreover, Brazil's huge investment in transportation infrastructure has been based on the automobile industry. A reorientation of policy—emphasizing alternative modes of transportation—must consequently threaten the usage of industrial and infrastructure capacity built around the automobile. It remains to be seen to what extent the Brazilian economy is now locked into a productive structure whose viability has been placed in question by the change in the relative price of its basic input. The extent to which the problem could be resolved by increased domestic production of petroleum is speculative. Brazil only produced 20 percent of its needs in the mid-1970s and the rate of growth of its discoveries of new oil sources has barely maintained that proportion. Whether the decision to allow foreign companies to explore Brazil's territory for oil under risk contracts will accelerate discoveries is also a matter of conjecture.

In early 1975 the Brazilian government recognized the distributional problem by raising minimum wages not only on grounds of equity but also because of the need to broaden the market for consumer goods. This policy was emphasized in late 1975 as the balance-of-payments crisis worsened. The reasoning for the continuation of policies designed to counter the concentration in the distribution of income is based not only on the need to broaden the market, but also on the need to minimize imports. It is said that by boosting the income of the lower income groups, demand for the products of traditional industries will increase. These industries have a lower import content than the industries producing many of the consumer durable goods and their promotion is thus desirable.

It would be ironic if the international crisis forced Brazil to reorient its development priorities and thus produced a growth process which will be more egalitarian in nature than the growth of the past.

3

BRAZIL'S EMERGING INTERNATIONAL ECONOMIC ROLE

William R. Cline

This essay examines the growing importance of Brazil in an economically interdependent world. It first considers the evolution, current difficulties, and future prospects of Brazil's foreign economic sector and then evaluates Brazil's role in the ongoing process of structural change in the international economy, with particular attention paid to the relationships between the rich and the poor countries.

Brazil's External Economic Sector

Autarchy or the Open Economy. Throughout the postwar period, until about 1967, Brazil pursued the strategy of import substitution industrialization. As a result its economy became more and more closed. As is shown in Table 1, imports as a share of gross domestic product declined from an early postwar average of 12 percent to a low of slightly over 5 percent in the 1964-67 period. The economy was even more closed in the final years of this long phase than it had been during the years of World War II, when supplies of imports were extremely scarce; and it was far more closed than during the depression years of the 1930s, when domestic industrialization received the strong stimulus of a lack of export earnings for the purchase of traditional imports.

During the two decades following World War II, the foreign sector's weight declined not only because attention was focused on the construction of domestic industry, but also because of a growing lethargy in exports. A general bias against the export of raw materials prevailed, as did a willingness to interrupt export supply whenever domestic inflationary problems made intervention convenient.[1]

---

[1] See Mario Henrique Simonsen, *Brasil 2001* (Rio de Janeiro: APEC, 1969), pp. 156-159.

Table 1
IMPORTS (CIF) AS A SHARE OF GROSS DOMESTIC
PRODUCT: BRAZIL, 1920–1974

Year	Percentage Share	Year	Percentage Share
1920–29	22.4	1961	7.3
1930–39	12.8	1962	7.0
1940–46	7.2	1963	6.7
1947–50	12.0	1964	5.6
1951	16.3	1965	4.5
1952	14.1	1966	5.6
1953	9.4	1967	5.9
1954	11.7	1968	6.8
1955	8.7	1969	6.7
1956	8.4	1970	6.2
1957	9.6	1971	7.0
1958	8.5	1972	7.8
1959	8.8	1973	9.0
1960	8.2	1974	13.7

Source: For 1920-67, Mario Simonsen, *Brasil 2001* (Rio de Janeiro: APEC, 1969), pp. 154-155; for 1968-74, International Monetary Fund, *International Financial Statistics,* various issues. 1974 estimate for GDP based on 1973 level plus 9.6 percent real growth and 31.75 percent inflation (*Conjuntura Econômica,* January 1975).

The years 1967 and 1968 represented a watershed in Brazilian economic history. By then it was evident that import substitution as a motor force for development had practically run its course and that a new emphasis on export growth was essential. In 1969 a tariff reform reduced the protection of Brazilian industry, changing the incentives so that producers would turn away from the domestic market and thus toward exports. In 1968, the policy of frequent "mini-devaluations" replaced the traditional policy of holding untenable exchange rates until domestic inflation finally forced their periodic collapse. At the political level the measure of the nation's honor was redefined from the stability of the exchange rate to the magnitude of reserves; at the economic level exporters now had a much lower risk level associated with production for export because they no longer had to gamble on earning foreign exchange during a phase of the exchange rate cycle when the rate was artificially unfavorable to them.

Supplementing lower protection and exchange rate realism was a structure of tax incentives for exports, eventually followed by a massive mercantile assault on world markets through foreign trade fairs and other marketing efforts. True to Brazilian form, the result of all of these measures was miraculous. Table 2 shows the growth rates for Brazilian exports during the past decade, and it is clear that from 1968 through 1974 there was a very heady acceleration. Nor was the boom solely due to world inflation in commodity prices, although that boosted export growth in 1973 and 1974. The rapid and persistent expansion of manufactured exports indicates that the export drive represented much more than a windfall gain from commodity inflation.

Overall, the aggressive export policies beginning in the late 1960s reopened the Brazilian economy to much higher levels of trade relative to the national product. Thus, by 1973, imports as a fraction of gross domestic product were twice their level at the low point in 1965, and by 1974 the import share was three times as high as in 1965, standing almost at 14 percent (Table 1)—or approximately twice the level for the United States or for the European Economic Community considered as a single unit.

Current Problems

Seven fat years of external economic boom gave way to lean years beginning in 1974 and (especially) 1975. Increased petroleum import prices raised Brazil's imported oil bill from $710 million in 1973 to $2.8 billion in 1974.[2] With export earnings and foreign reserves buoyed by sharp price increases for Brazil's own commodity exports, and with access to credits from abroad, the oil shock itself was manageable. However, the overall import bill skyrocketed in 1974 (rising from $6.2 billion to $12.6 billion FOB).[3] The increase in imports far exceeded both the extra cost of oil and the increase in export earnings for the year. Three principal elements explain the large increase in imports in 1974: increases in prices of imported industrial goods (as double-digit inflation spread through the industrial world), continued rapid domestic growth, and a lagging of the exchange rate behind the pace of devaluation that would have been indicated by the ratio of domestic inflation to international inflation. Overextension in 1974 was followed by stagnation in world markets in 1975 as the industrial countries went simultaneously into a recession sharper than any since the 1930s. The end result was extraordinarily

---

[2] Banco Central do Brasil, *Boletim*, vol. 12, no. 1 (January 1976), p. 207.
[3] Ibid.

Table 2

BRAZILIAN EXPORTS, TOTAL AND MAJOR PRODUCTS, 1964–1975

(US $ millions)

Year	Total	Percent Growth	Coffee	Iron Ore	Sugar	Soybeans		Manufactured Goods
						Grain	Cakes and bran	
1964	1,429.8	...	759.9	80.6	33.0	...	3.0	89.3
1965	1,595.5	11.6	707.4	103.0	56.7	7.3	7.7	129.0
1966	1,741.4	9.1	773.5	100.2	80.5	13.0	14.6	142.5
1967	1,654.0	−5.0	733.0	102.8	80.4	29.2	10.2	163.8
1968	1,881.3	13.7	797.3	104.5	101.6	6.3	18.9	175.9
1969	2,311.2	22.8	845.7	147.4	115.0	29.2	23.4	244.7
1970	2,738.9	18.5	981.8	209.6	126.6	27.1	43.6	365.7
1971	2,903.9	6.0	822.2	237.3	153.0	24.3	81.5	522.0
1972	3,991.2	37.4	1,057.1	231.7	403.5	127.9	152.3	830.3
1973	6,199.2	55.3	1,344.2	362.8	552.7	494.2	422.6	1,134.4
1974	7,951.0	28.3	980.4	571.2	1,261.6	586.3	303.0	2,146.7
1975[a]	8,947.0	13.7	903.4	899.9	1,197.9	697.1	505.5	2,411.7

[a] Actual figures available for January–November only. Estimate equals 1974 figure multiplied by 1975-to-1974 ratio for first eleven months.

Source: Banco Central do Brasil, *Boletim*, vol. 12, no. 1 (January 1976), pp. 202–205.

large trade deficits in 1974 and 1975 and a correspondingly large increase in the already high level of foreign indebtedness. To make matters worse, raw materials export prices began backing off from their mid-1974 peaks, although they remained high enough to make the terms of trade much more favorable than they had been in (say) 1971, before the early 1970s phase of world commodity price inflation. The very success of earlier import substitution industrialization meant that remaining imports were rigid and essential to ongoing growth. Of total imports, consumer nondurables represented only 1.1 percent and consumer durables only 6.1 percent in 1974;[4] the remaining imports were intermediate goods or capital goods essential for production and growth. The need to constrain imports after their enormous surge in 1974 and in the face of a slowdown in export expansion undoubtedly contributed to the deceleration of real growth in 1975 and (very probably) in 1976.

It is important to give detailed consideration to two aspects of the external economic sector: foreign exchange rate policy and external debt. The policy of exchange rate realism since the late 1960s has meant that the cruzeiro has devalued at a rate approximately equal to the rate of difference between Brazilian inflation and inflation in U.S. dollar prices. A closer examination of devaluation permits an assessment of its role in the developments described above.

Although inadequate for precise determination of the appropriate exchange rate, "purchasing power parity" analysis does permit a general examination of the extent to which a currency has been kept at reasonable exchange rates. Given the rate of inflation of an appropriate U.S. price index (the wholesale price index) and the rate for the corresponding Brazilian index, the percentage devaluation of the cruzeiro vis-à-vis the dollar should equal the difference between the two (divided by a figure equal to unity plus the Brazilian inflation rate).[5] To be sure, other factors are omitted from a simple comparison

---

[4] Confederação Nacional do Comércio, *A Economia Brasileira: Sumário 1974* (Rio de Janeiro, March 1975).

[5] Let R be the exchange rate, dollars per cruzeiro. Let P be price, subscript c refer to cruzeiro prices, subscript d refer to dollar prices, superscript o refer to base year, superscript 1 to terminal year, and the "dotted" variable be the proportional change in the variable indicated. In order to maintain constant purchasing power parity, at all times the ratio of cruzeiro to dollar prices should equal the reciprocal of the exchange rate.
From the above definitions,

$$P_c/P_d = 1/R \qquad (1)$$

$$P_c^1 = P_c^o(1 + \dot{P}_c); \ P_d^1 = P_d^o(1 + \dot{P}_d); \ R^1 = R^o(1 + \dot{R}) \qquad (2)$$

of this sort. In particular, the devaluation of the dollar itself vis-à-vis other major currencies in 1971 and 1973 raises the question whether additional account should be taken of other currencies, although to the extent that the dollar devalued because of U.S. inflation greater than that in Europe and Japan, the relevant information for calculating the appropriate exchange rate would already be included in the figure for U.S. inflation.

Table 3 presents data on devaluation of the cruzeiro from 1961 through 1975. Column (5) shows the actual percentage change in the dollar/cruzeiro rate and column (6) the change that would have been recommended on the basis of the purchasing power parity approach. A serious limitation of the analysis is that it assumes for each year that the prior year was an equilibrium base, so that, for a long series of years in which actual devaluation is smaller than recommended, the cumulative overvaluation by the end of the period is much greater than what is suggested by the difference between actual and recommended devaluation in that year alone.

Columns (5) and (6) of Table 3 indicate the following patterns: Before the military revolution, devaluation kept approximate pace with the "appropriate" rates in 1961 and 1962 but fell behind in 1963. By contrast, massive devaluation in 1964 probably reestablished a realistic exchange rate. However, over the next three years cruzeiro devaluation lagged seriously behind the rate indicated by relative inflation in Brazil and the United States. In 1968, the first year of the policy of mini-devaluation, the situation again appears to have been rectified (inasmuch as devaluation for the year exceeded the purchasing parity indicator, thereby regaining ground lost in previous years).

For the 1969-73 period, the table indicates an uninterrupted pattern of modestly lagging cruzeiro devaluation. Each year the per-

---

For purchasing parity to remain constant,

$$P_c^1/P_d^1 = 1/R^1 = P_c^o/P_d^o = 1/R^o \qquad (3)$$

So that:

$$\frac{P_c^o(1 + \dot{P}_c)}{P_d^o(1 + \dot{P}_d)} = 1/[R^o(1+\dot{R})] \qquad (4)$$

Dividing both sides by R^o (or its equivalent, P_c^o/P_d^o) and rearranging,

$$1 + \dot{P}_c + \dot{R} + \dot{R}\dot{P}_c = 1 + \dot{P}_d \qquad (5)$$

and

$$\dot{R} = [\dot{P}_d - \dot{P}_c]/[1 + \dot{P}_c] \qquad (6)$$

For example, if Brazilian inflation is 25 percent and U.S. inflation is 10 percent, the proportional change in the dollar/cruzeiro rate should be: $\underline{.10 - .25} = -.12$, or there should be a 12 percent devaluation. $\qquad 1.25$

Table 3
PRICES, DEVALUATION, AND PURCHASING POWER PARITY: BRAZIL, 1960–1975

Year	Percent Inflation, Brazil (1)	Percent Inflation, U.S. (2)	Exchange Rate, Cruzeiro/$ (3)	Exchange Rate, $/New Cruzeiro (4)	Percent Change of Exchange Rate (5)	Percent Change of Exchange Rate (Hypothetical) to Maintain Purchasing Parity (6)	Reserves ($ millions end of year) (7)
1960	...	...	205.1	4.88	...	...	345
1961	39.9	0	318.5	3.14	−35.7	−28.5	470
1962	50.6	0	475.0	2.11	−32.8	−33.6	291
1963	76.0	0	620.0	1.61	−23.7	−43.2	219
1964	82.2	2.0	1,850.0	.54	−66.5	−45.1	245
1965	52.7	3.9	2,220.0	.45	−16.7	−33.2	484
1966	42.4	0	2,220.0	.45	0	−27.0	425
1967	25.3	1.9	2.715	.368	−18.2	−20.2	199
1968	24.0	4.4	3.830	.261	−29.1	−17.8	257
1969	20.2	4.4	4.350	.230	−11.9	−13.1	657
1970	22.1	3.6	4.950	.202	−12.2	−15.2	1,187
1971	20.5	3.3	5.635	.178	−12.1	−14.3	1,746
1972	18.4	4.5	6.215	.161	−9.4	−11.7	4,183
1973	16.1	13.1	6.220	.161	−0.1	−2.6	6,416
1974	29.5	18.9	7.435	.135	−16.4	−8.2	5,251
1975	25.1 a	9.1	8.775 b	.114	−15.2	−12.8	4,190 c

Notes: Column (1): Wholesale prices excluding coffee. Column (2): Wholesale prices. Column (4): Free rate. Prices: Average for year. Exchange rate: End of year. Column (6): Equals [(2) − (1)]/[1 + (1)] where columns (1) and (2) are expressed as proportions.
a End of June 1975.
b End of November 1975.
c As of May 1975.
Source: Calculated from International Monetary Fund, *International Financial Statistics*, selected issues.

centage devaluation was two to three percentage points below "appropriate" levels, suggesting that by the end of the period the cruzeiro had once again become seriously overvalued. It is noteworthy that during this same period, as shown in the table, foreign exchange reserves grew by very large amounts. The appearance of ample reserves may well have contributed to the exchange rate policy leading to overvaluation of the cruzeiro. This assessment, if correct, is especially relevant when the relationship of reserves to growing foreign debt is considered; to some extent the growth of reserves, if taken as an indication of external economic strength, was illusory, since much of it was in a sense mortgaged and represented little more than the collateral on the basis of which were contracted much larger loans from abroad.

In 1974 and 1975 exchange rate policy reversed, and the degree of devaluation exceeded that indicated by the maintenance of purchasing power parity from one year to the next, permitting a partial reestablishment of exchange rate realism after gradually growing overvaluation during the previous five years.

In sum, analysis of the exchange rate over time suggests that a substantial part of Brazil's emerging problem with the foreign sector in 1974 and 1975 was attributable to an overvalued exchange rate. This diagnosis is consistent with the fact that the surge in imports in 1974 far exceeded what could be explained by the increased cost of oil, and that the single policy with the broadest general impact on imports is exchange rate policy.

There is another and more subtle aspect of exchange rate policy. Purchasing power parity can be an inappropriate guide to the exchange rate when fundamental changes take place in the foreign sector. Brazilian authorities generally have followed a purchasing parity approach in mini-devaluations of the cruzeiro (even though the data here suggest they did so to an insufficient degree). But there is the danger that a strict adherence to such a policy can introduce a new type of exchange rate rigidity—an inflexibility in the extent to which devaluation *in real terms* can be employed when changes in the trading and capital flow situations require change. Moreover, a number of Brazilian financial instruments appear to have been used by investors under expectations of a rigid continuing relationship between the rate of devaluation and the relative inflation rate, and it is possible that authorities believe themselves to be constrained in any departure from the past relationship because they believe there would be severe negative repercussions in the financial

Table 4

GROWTH OF BRAZIL'S EXTERNAL DEBT, 1969–1975

Year	Debt Outstanding, End of Year (US $ millions)	Percentage Growth Rate from Prior Year
1969	4,403.3	...
1970	5,295.2	20.3
1971	6,621.6	25.0
1972	9,521.0	43.8
1973	12,571.0	32.0
1974	17,165.7	36.5
1975	22,000.0	28.2

Source: "Dívida Externa Brasileira: Algumas Considerações," *Conjuntura Econômica*, vol. 30, no. 4 (April 1976), p. 76.

markets.[6] The overall result may be a paradoxically rigid *real* exchange rate despite the appearance of a sophisticated degree of flexibility in exchange rate policy.

Another area which warrants detailed examination is the problem of external debt. It is well known that external capital played a crucial role in Brazil's economic "miracle" of the late 1960s and early 1970s. What is perhaps less well known is that the bulk of the foreign capital entered as loans rather than direct private investment, and that as a result Brazil has accumulated an extremely large foreign debt. Table 4 shows, for 1969 through 1975, the rapid growth and massive amount of Brazil's external debt.

The rapid accumulation of enormous foreign indebtedness makes the stimulation of export earnings and the moderation of import growth a matter of urgency even greater than might be inferred from trade and balance-of-payments figures alone. The large outstanding debt means that a large portion of each year's export earnings is earmarked for the payment of interest and amortization. It also means that further drawing on foreign credit becomes more and more problematical, even though Brazil enjoys a relatively strong credit rating in qualitative terms.

To assess the seriousness of the debt problem in quantitative terms, it may be useful to employ a statistical model of credit-

---

[6] This concern may apply to Brazilian private borrowings on the Eurodollar market.

worthiness from an earlier study of debt rescheduling among developing countries.[7] In this study, discriminant analysis was used to determine threshold levels of debt-servicing difficulties, beyond which developing countries had generally been forced to reschedule their debt in the past. The method separates countries (for a given year) into two groups: those likely to reschedule and those not. The best statistical results were obtained using relatively simple models. One of the models used only two variables—the debt service ratio (ratio of interest and amortization payments to export earnings [merchandise trade]) and the ratio of amortization to outstanding debt—an indicator of the speed with which debt is being reduced and therefore whether any problem is longer term or merely a short-run difficulty. Another model added a third variable—the ratio of imports to reserves (the higher the ratio, the more unfavorable the creditworthiness of the country). Naming these three indicators X_1, X_2, and X_3 respectively, we find that the best statistical results were obtained with the following equations:

$Z_1 = 27.285\ X_1 - 20.38\ X_2$, with the critical value of Z_1 being 3.437; and $Z_2 = 26.779\ X_1 - 24.824\ X_2 + 0.702\ X_3$, with the critical value of 6.412.[8]

The data underlying these models referred to public and publicly guaranteed debt only (of one year maturity or greater). In Brazil, however, there are relatively large amounts of private external debt. If one considers the debt service ratio including service payments on all debt, both public and private, then Brazil appears to be in serious debt difficulties indeed: this debt service ratio was 41 percent in 1975,[9] whereas 20 percent is normally considered a dangerously high debt service ratio. However, for assessment using standard indicators based on international experience, it is necessary to examine the data referring to public and publicly guaranteed debt. The relevant estimates appear in Table 5, and the methods of estimation are described in the notes to the table.

As shown in the table, the debt service ratio on public and publicly guaranteed debt alone was reaching an uncomfortably high

---

[7] Charles R. Frank, Jr. and William R. Cline, "Measurement of Debt-Servicing Capacity: An Application of Discriminant Analysis," *Journal of International Economics*, vol. 1, no. 3 (1971), pp. 327-344.

[8] Ibid., p. 337.

[9] "Dívida Externa Brasileira: Algumas Considerações," *Conjuntura Econômica*, vol. 30, no. 4 (April 1976), p. 78. The corresponding debt service ratios for 1968 through 1974 were, respectively, 51 percent, 54 percent, 54 percent, 58 percent, 42 percent, and 33 percent.

Table 5

ESTIMATED PUBLIC AND PUBLICLY GUARANTEED
EXTERNAL DEBT, DEBT SERVICE, AND INDICATORS OF
DEBT SERVICING CAPACITY: BRAZIL, 1975 AND 1976

($ millions)

	1975	1976
A. Public, publicly guaranteed external debt, beginning of year [a]	8,772	11,242
B. Interest [b]	652	835
C. Amortization [c]	766	981
D. Debt Service (B + C)	1,418	1,816
E. Exports [d]	8,655	9,520
F. Debt service ratio (D/E)	.164	.191
G. Reserves, beginning of year [e]	5,251	4,013
H. Imports [f]	13,558	14,000
I. Imports/Reserves (H/G)	2.582	3.489
J. Two-variable credit-worthiness indicator (Z_1) (critical value: 3.437) [g]	2.690	3.427
K. Three-variable credit-worthiness indicator (Z_2) (critical value: 6.412) [h]	4.032	5.392

Sources and notes:

[a] Estimated as 51.1 percent of total external debt (Table 4 shows *end* of year total debt). This ratio is based on table 4 and on the figure reported for public and publicly guaranteed debt at the end of 1973 (net of undisbursed) in: International Bank for Reconstruction and Development, *World Debt Tables: Volume I, External Public Debt of LDCs,* EC-167/75 (Washington, D.C.: IBRD, 1975), p. 4. Informed opinion is that the ratio of public and publicly guaranteed debt to total debt has not changed substantially since the end of 1973.

[b] Estimated as 7.43 percent of debt outstanding at beginning of year. This average interest rate is reported for Brazil's public external debt acquired in the period 1971-73. IBRD, *World Debt Tables: Volume II, External Debt of LDCs,* EC-167/75 (Washington, D.C.: IBRD, 1975), p. 183.

[c] Estimated as 8.73 percent of debt outstanding at beginning of year. This is the ratio of 1973 amortization to beginning of year public debt, as reported in IBRD, *World Debt Tables . . . Volume I,* pp. 4, 10.

[d] 1975: International Monetary Fund, *International Financial Statistics,* vol. 29, no. 4 (April 1976), p. 38. 1976: estimated as 10 percent above 1975.

[e] *International Financial Statistics* (April 1976), p. 19.

[f] 1975: *International Financial Statistics* (April 1976), p. 39. 1976: round figure estimate assuming success with programs limiting import expansion. Note that 1974 imports were $14,162 million. Ibid.

[g] See text.

[h] See text.

level of 19 percent in 1976. Indeed, the statistical indicator based on debt service ratio and amortization rate shows the 1975 measure below the "critical" value associated with debt rescheduling but the 1976 expected level almost exactly equal to this critical level (line J in the table). Once Brazil's relatively ample reserves are taken into account using the three-variable model (which includes the imports/ reserves variable), the indicator for 1976 falls somewhat below the critical level.

In short, using statistically estimated models of the severity of external debt problems, Brazil appears to be close to, but not beyond, levels of debt servicing burdens (on public and publicly guaranteed debt) associated in the past with debt reschedulings in diverse developing countries. Extreme caution in the debt area is therefore in order. This conclusion is strongly reinforced by the fact that Brazil has an unusually high private foreign debt (in relative and absolute terms), so that if the debt situation is close to dangerous for public and publicly guaranteed debt alone, it is all the more precarious when private debt is taken into account as well.

To be sure, at this point foreign creditors may have little option beyond the further extension of credit. But the data and analysis here suggest that, at the very least, a priority item in Brazil's external economic policy must be a sharp reduction in the rate of expansion of foreign debt. The corresponding implication is, once again, that there is a heightened need to stimulate exports and moderate the growth of imports.

The policy response to foreign sector difficulties in 1974 and 1975 appears to have represented a major turning point in Brazilian economic strategy. Devaluation of the exchange rate has been used relatively little, although in 1974 and 1975 the pace of mini-devaluations accelerated enough to reverse the previous pattern where devaluation lagged behind the differential between cruzeiro and dollar inflation (Table 3). Instead, especially in the latter part of 1975, the Brazilian government turned to policies of import restriction. Tariffs were increased, as were advance deposits required for importation (which represent a disguised tariff because of the decline in real value of monetary deposits during the time they are held idle). It is too early to tell whether the resort to protectionist measures associated with Brazil's earlier phase of import substitution represents a new withdrawal from the outward-looking growth strategy that began in the mid-1960s. However, much is at stake; an entire development approach stands in question because of the new pressure on Brazil's external economic sector. In the near term the outcome of the crisis will probably depend to an important degree on the extent to which Brazil's exports expand as the industrial world pulls out of its severe 1974-75 recession.

Long-Run Prospects

In a longer term perspective it is not surprising that the growth of Brazil's foreign sector should be decelerating. If the rapid rise in the openness of the economy beginning in 1968 is kept in mind, the rapid growth of exports and imports in this period may be seen as a transitional phenomenon accompanying the rise in the economy's openness from a low to an intermediate (or relatively high) plateau. Sustainable long-run growth rates in the foreign sector are therefore quite probably well below the average rates in the period 1968-73. The openness of the economy is already well above that for the United States (7 percent), the European Economic Community as a group, and Japan (both 9 percent).[10] If the figure for imports as a fraction of national product stabilizes, then the growth rate of the foreign sector cannot exceed that of overall national product, which would be expected to be 10 percent or less annually in real terms.[11]

Even so, the long-run prospects for Brazilian exports look bright. Coffee is no longer the key export; by 1975 manufactured goods had risen to 28 percent of total exports (Table 2)—although some observers note that the manufactured goods exported have slowly growing world markets.[12] Prospects for future expansion of manufactured exports would seem good, both for the Latin American market and to the rest of the world. However, there are danger signals. Brazil's exports of textiles come under the general multifiber agreement limiting textile exports under "voluntary" quotas. Brazil's exports of shoes to the United States have been placed under "countervailing duty" action, whereby an additional tariff is charged to compensate for subsidies to exports from the government of the supplying country. There are other important manufactured goods sectors with possible longer-run problems. Brazil might be expected to develop comparative advantage for exporting steel, in view of the country's iron ore

---

[10] C. Fred Bergsten and William R. Cline, "Increasing International Economic Interdependence: The Implications for Research," *American Economic Review*, vol. 66, no. 2 (May 1976), p. 155.

[11] However, even within these restrictions exports could grow at a faster rate in order to close the gap between imports and exports.

[12] Werner Baer, "The Brazilian Boom, 1968-72: An Explanation and Interpretation," *World Development*, vol. 1, no. 8 (1973), p. 13.

reserves and in light of the vigorous program of steel capacity expansion (despite current net importation of steel). Yet it is not unlikely that strong pressures for the protection of steel in industrial countries will close the doors of those countries to this product just as they were closed to textiles. The perceived threat in fact appears to be the same: the rapidly expanding export capacity of the developing countries and corresponding penetration of domestic markets in the rich countries.

Brazil's abundant natural resources represent the trump card for its future external economic prospects. Even after abatement of the seeming crises of resource supply associated with the rampant commodity inflation of 1973 and 1974, the world economy appears to be in a long-term seller's market for natural resources. Economists are shelving the assessments of Nurkse, Prebisch, and other analysts who a quarter of a century ago foresaw continuing stagnation in raw materials prices because of demand that was inelastic with respect to income and because of substitution by synthetic products. Instead, they are rereading the theory of exhaustible resources,[13] which calls for the real rent of non-replaceable resources to rise at an annual rate equal to the interest rate; and, if not convinced, they are at least disconcerted by the "doomsday" models forecasting worldwide economic collapse for lack of natural resources.

The humble soybean illustrates Brazil's stake in the raw materials game. When the United States imposed export controls on soybeans to fight domestic inflation, Japan and European countries turned to Brazil as an alternate source of supply. The result, as shown in Table 2, was a tenfold rise in the value of Brazil's soybean exports between 1971 and 1975 (reaching $1.2 billion in 1975). Again, sugar's spiraling price boosted Brazil's earnings from sugar exports by practically the same amount over the same period.

For long-run agricultural exports in general, Brazil's comparative advantage appears strong. This is especially true if areas not currently in agricultural establishments, including much of the Amazon basin, are counted as having long-run agricultural potential.[14]

---

[13] Harold Hotelling, "The Economics of Exhaustible Resources," *Journal of Political Economy*, vol. 39, no. 2 (April 1931), pp. 137-175.

[14] On the basis of total land area per agricultural population, Brazil (with 21.0 hectares per person) ranks sixth among thirty major developing countries (behind Argentina, Bolivia, Uruguay, Venezuela, and Chile). On the basis of agricultural land area per agricultural population, Brazil (with 3.48 hectares per person) ranks eighth. See R. Albert Berry and William R. Cline, "Farm Size, Factor Productivity and Technical Change" (Washington, D.C., 1976, processed), p. D-5.

Among minerals, Brazil's position in iron ore is especially strong, accounting for 15 percent of world reserves.[15] At the present time, however, Brazil's position is much less favorable than this in petroleum and in copper, coal, tin, and other minerals. However, the Brazilian government is embarked on a program of rapid development of mining (and eventually, processing) in bauxite (for which the electricity needed to make aluminum should come on stream with the joint Brazil-Paraguay Itaipu system) and other metals.[16] Moreover, it is at least possible that with the more liberalized treatment of foreign companies in oil exploration, Brazil's dependence on foreign petroleum will decline.

Overall, Brazil's long-run export prospects must be considered strong. The foreign sector problems of 1974 and 1975 seem likely to be overcome by longer run dynamism of exports, even though the heady pace of export expansion between 1967 and 1973 is unlikely to continue over the longer term—if only because the result would be an improbably high degree of openness of the economy.

Brazil's International Economic Role

This survey of Brazil's foreign economic sector shows transitional problems of excessive debt, imports temporarily out of control (perhaps because of creeping overvaluation of the cruzeiro), and a slackening of the country's high export growth rates; but, despite these temporary problems, it also shows long-run strength in the foreign sector. With this evaluation as background, we may turn to Brazil's international economic role, considering its importance relative to other developing countries and its potential for policy leadership among the developing countries.

Brazil's Economic Importance. To obtain an idea of the relative weight of Brazil on the international economic scene, it is useful to consider international data on foreign trade. Table 6 presents data for 1968 through 1974 on exports and foreign reserves of all developing countries, of oil-exporting developing countries, and of Brazil, as well as the ratios of the figures for Brazil to those for alternative groupings of developing countries. Table 7 presents data on exports and imports for twenty developing countries, ranking the countries by dollar value of exports and imports.

---

[15] Joseph Grunwald and Philip Musgrove, *Natural Resources in Latin American Development* (Baltimore: Johns Hopkins University Press, 1970), p. 116.

[16] H. J. Maidenberg, "Brazil's Underground Riches," *New York Times*, February 29, 1976, p. F-3.

Table 6
EXPORTS AND RESERVES: BRAZIL COMPARED WITH ALL LESS-DEVELOPED COUNTRIES, 1968–1974

Year	All LDCs (1)	Oil Export-ing LDCs (2)	Non-oil Export-ing LDCs (3)	Brazil (4)	Brazil as Percent of Total (5)	Brazil as Percent of Non-oil LDCs (6)
			I. Exports ($ millions)			
1968	42,900	14,700	28,200	1,881	4.4	6.7
1969	48,300	16,100	32,200	2,311	4.8	7.2
1970	54,200	18,300	35,900	2,739	5.1	7.6
1971	61,500	24,200	37,300	2,904	4.7	7.8
1972	73,400	28,700	44,700	3,991	5.4	8.9
1973	109,900	44,800	65,100	6,199	5.6	9.5
1974	225,800	136,300	89,500	7,951	3.5	8.9
			II. Reserves ($ millions)			
1970	18,871	5,226	13,646	1,187	6.3	8.7
1971	24,174	8,697	15,477	1,746	7.2	11.3
1972	32,200	11,220	20,980	4,183	13.0	19.9
1973	44,146	14,933	29,213	6,416	14.5	22.0
1974	79,615	48,007	31,608	5,251	6.6	16.6

Source: International Monetary Fund, *International Financial Statistics*, vol. 29, no. 1 (January 1976), pp. 38, 19.

As is shown in Table 6, as late as 1973 Brazil's exports amounted to close to 6 percent of the total for all developing countries. By 1974, the first year showing the full impact of the increase in oil prices, Brazil's export share had fallen to 3.5 percent, although it stood at approximately 9 percent if we consider non-oil-exporting developing countries only. Brazil's share in LDC reserves has been even greater, peaking in 1973 at 14.5 percent of the total including oil-exporting countries and at 22 percent of the sum for non-oil-exporting LDCs only. These percentage shares indicate Brazil's major importance among the developing countries, although they do not indicate as predominant a role as the United States plays among the industrial countries. (In 1974 U.S. exports were approximately one-fifth of the total for industrial countries.) [17]

[17] International Monetary Fund, *International Financial Statistics*, vol. 29, no. 1 (January 1976), p. 38.

Table 7
RANKINGS OF DEVELOPING COUNTRIES BY DOLLAR VALUES OF EXPORTS AND IMPORTS

Country	Exports 1974 (in million U.S. $ with rank)	Exports 1968 (in million U.S. $ with rank)	Imports 1974 (in million U.S. $ with rank)
1. Saudi Arabia	35,657	2,026 (2)	1,865 (18)
2. Iran	24,002	1,881 (3)	5,672 (7)
3. Kuwait	10,957	1,437 (8)	1,552 (20)
4. Venezuela	10,732	2,506 (1)	4,200 (10)
5. Nigeria	9,567	591 (18)	2,737 (16)
6. Libya	8,259	1,863 (5)	2,763 (15)
7. Iraq	8,177	1,039 (13)	2,273 (17)
8. Brazil	7,951 [1]	1,881 (4)	14,162 (1)
9. Indonesia	7,426	731 (17)	5,672 (8)
10. United Arab Emirates	7,371	340 (20)	1,605 (19)
11. Hong Kong	5,959 [2]	1,744 (7)	6,768 (5)
12. Singapore	5,811 [3]	1,271 (11)	8,380 (2)
13. Taiwan	5,533 [4]	789 (16)	6,964 (3)
14. Korea	4,461 [5]	455 (19)	6,844 (4)
15. Algeria	4,336	830 (15)	4,058 (12)
16. Malaysia	4,233 [6]	1,347 (10)	4,155 (11)
17. Argentina	3,932 [7]	1,368 (9)	3,570 (13)
18. India	3,927 [8]	1,761 (6)	5,043 (9)
19. Mexico	3,540 [9]	1,254 (12)	6,504 (6)
20. Philippines	2,671 [10]	857 (14)	3,436 (14)

Source: International Monetary Fund, *International Financial Statistics*, vol. 29, no. 1 (January 1976), pp. 38-41.

The rankings shown in Table 7 confirm Brazil's importance. By value of exports Brazil ranked fourth in 1968 but eighth by 1974 because of the dramatic rise in oil exports. However, among non-oil-exporting countries, Brazil stood first by value of exports in 1974. Moreover, in total imports, Brazil ranked first of all of the developing countries in 1974, surpassing even the oil-rich countries. Undoubtedly rapid growth of imports for certain oil-exporting countries (such as Iran) will place Brazil behind them in value of imports in the intermediate term. However, the main message of the data is that Brazil ranks first among the non-oil LDCs in the magnitude of its external economic sector and even outranks the major oil-exporting countries in the size of the import market it presents to the world. This primacy is all the more impressive when it is kept in mind that Brazil's economy is much more closed than are those of other countries with large export magnitudes (such as Hong Kong, Singapore, Taiwan, and South Korea).

Of course, population is another criterion for international economic importance. India counts for more in the international economic system (especially in its bargaining processes) than does Singapore, even though India's exports are only two-thirds the value of Singapore's. However, on this standard as well Brazil ranks high among developing countries, with its population exceeded only by those of India and Indonesia.

In light of the primacy (or at least very high ranking) of Brazil's foreign economic sector among developing countries, the country's "importance" in the international economic system is indisputable. What is more ambiguous is what this importance implies for Brazil's policy role vis-à-vis other developing countries on the one hand and the industrial countries on the other. Brazil's very size and dynamism make it a logical candidate for international economic leadership of the developing countries. But the same size and dynamism also make Brazil something of a threat to other potential leading countries, particularly within Latin America. The perception of this threat of economic influence has been increased by some specific economic policies in recent years—such policies as the extension of Brazilian credit for exports to smaller neighboring Latin American countries, and "joint projects" with some of the same countries, especially with Bolivia and Paraguay. Still another possible limitation on Brazil's leadership role—again paradoxically related to her very size and success—is the fact that the country is much richer than the "fourth world" of truly impoverished countries—India, Bangladesh, many African countries, and (in the Western Hemisphere) Haiti. Thus, while neighbors' fears of Brazilian influence and expansion tend to limit Brazil's leadership role within the Western Hemisphere, the gulf between Brazil's "international middle class" status and the extreme poverty of the fourth world limits that role in the broader context of all developing countries. Measures aimed directly at the poorest countries (such as the per capita income ceiling on recipient countries in the International Development Association [$375] and the new IMF Trust Fund financed by gold sales [300 SDRs] tend to omit Brazil and other middle-income countries, creating the potential for divergence of interest between the two types of developing countries.

Nevertheless, Brazil quite clearly has increasingly been playing a leadership role in the international economic system. In order to document this role, it is necessary to consider Brazil's part in recent international economic negotiations, as well as the country's likely role in forthcoming negotiations.

Monetary Reform Negotiations.[18] The collapse of the Bretton Woods system of fixed exchange rates and convertibility of the dollar into gold in the period 1971-73 set the stage for the most significant set of international economic negotiations since World War II. These negotiations have been especially significant from the standpoint of the developing countries. Whereas the LDCs had generally had little voice in international economic arrangements (such as the Kennedy Round of trade negotiations, and various Group of Ten ad hoc monetary swap arrangements), they demanded and received full representation in the formal negotiating bodies established in the International Monetary Fund to draw up new rules for the international monetary system.

In 1972 the "Committee of Twenty" of the IMF began monetary reform negotiations. Developing countries accounted for nine of the twenty representatives, and Brazil was one of the nine developing countries directly represented in the committee. After the committee submitted its final (but inconclusive) report in mid-1974, subsequent negotiations took place in the IMF "Interim Committee" composed of the finance ministers of the same countries that had direct representatives in the Committee of Twenty.

One of the chief demands of the developing countries in the monetary reform negotiations was for a link between the issuance of special drawing rights (SDRs) and the provision of development assistance. The intensity of this demand appears to have diminished as it became clearer that (because of excess world liquidity) no SDRs would be created for several years. It is a mark of the pragmatism of the developing country participants in the monetary reform discussions (as opposed to the rhetorical emphasis of their participation in other forums such as successive UNCTAD meetings) that these participants went along with other important major reforms even though the question of the "link" was postponed. One of those other measures, the sale of a portion of the IMF's gold and the use of resulting profits for development aid through a trust fund, represented a concrete achievement for the developing countries—an achievement that, at least to some extent, appears to have compensated

---

[18] For a discussion of the developing countries' role in world monetary reform, see William R. Cline, *International Monetary Reform and the Developing Countries* (Washington, D.C.: Brookings Institution, 1976).

for failure to establish a link at the present time. We do not know the individual positions Brazil took on these issues, but it seems likely that Brazilian participation worked in the direction of setting a tone of pragmatism among the developing country representatives in the negotiating bodies.

Another important issue in monetary reform concerned the degree of flexibility of exchange rates. The developing countries initially tended to oppose greater flexibility of exchange rates among industrial countries, fearing that increased flexibility would cause new uncertainties in their own economic planning. After the movement to floating by major industrial countries in 1973, however, IMF rules requiring par values became an anachronism. It is the author's understanding that in the key negotiations leading to the Jamaica agreement (January 1976) legitimizing flexible rates (and providing for consultation procedures), Brazil provided important support for the U.S.-sponsored revisions allowing floating exchange rates (helping to offset demands by some European participants that any allowance for floating be specified as strictly temporary).

The process of monetary reform has marked what may be a major turning point for the developing countries in their active participation in the formation of the international economic system. It has already spawned new forums based on the same model of representation, including the International Monetary Fund-International Bank for Reconstruction and Development Committee on Transfer of Resources and the Paris-based Conference on International Economic Cooperation. Perhaps one of the most important precedents set by the monetary negotiations is that of representation roughly proportional to economic significance (along the general IMF lines). In contrast to the United Nations' one-nation, one-vote structure, the emergence of this pattern of negotiations bodes well for the practical establishment of new measures in the international economic system. And, from the parochial standpoint of Brazil's own role, the incorporation of economic weight into negotiating weight enhances that role in the process of international economic negotiations.

In sum, Brazil has played an important role in the negotiations on world monetary reform, in which the developing countries as a group have achieved important successes (undisputed right to participation and the concrete measure of aid through IMF gold sales) despite temporary defeat on an SDR aid link.[19]

---

[19] Note that as formulated by the developing countries in the Committee of Twenty, the link proposal could have been important for Brazil (once SDRs were again created) because distribution was to be based on IMF quotas. But

Trade Negotiations. The other major formal negotiations in process are in the "Tokyo Round" of multilateral trade negotiations. Although the developing countries are unlikely to offer significant reductions in their own protection in these negotiations, they still represent an important voice in the negotiation process, especially on general questions of the "equity" of the various alternative trade liberalization measures that the major industrial countries may negotiate. In particular, there are three broad areas in which the developing countries are interested. First, there are several non-tariff barrier issues on which negotiated agreements will affect them. Second, they stand to gain as "free-riders" from increased export opportunities as the industrial countries lower their tariffs across the board to all suppliers (so-called "most-favored-nation" tariff cuts). Third, there is the area of tariff preferences. There exists a concern among LDCs that general liberalization among industrial countries may be disadvantageous to the developing countries because declining tariffs would erode the special advantage conferred on the LDCs by free entry under tariff preferences.

For Brazil perhaps the most serious area of negotiation is that concerning non-tariff barriers. The application of U.S. countervailing duties on Brazilian shoes and Brazil's "voluntary" export restraints on textiles represent a serious threat to the future expansion of manufactured exports. The real danger is not in these particular products but in the specter of a proliferation of "voluntary export controls" in the future if the United States and other industrial countries feel threatened by rapidly growing industrial imports from the developing countries.

On the question of tariffs, Brazil stands to gain substantially from the "free rider" benefit. Preliminary calculations indicate that a 60 percent tariff cut by the industrial countries would increase Brazil's total exports by approximately $100 million annually.[20] Similarly, Brazil would participate in increased export opportunities over the longer run if the European Economic Community were to reduce its agricultural protection through variable levies.

---

in view of the strong movement of concessional aid vehicles toward strict concentration on the poorest countries, it is unlikely that a future "link," if adopted, would distribute aid according to IMF quotas among LDCs; instead, it very probably would go to the poorest countries, bypassing Brazil.

[20] For a description of the project in which these calculations are conducted, see William R. Cline, Noboru Kawanabe, T. O. M. Kronsjo, and Thomas Williams, "Trade, Welfare, and Employment Effects of Multilateral Trade Negotiations in the Tokyo Round" (Washington, D.C.: 1976, processed).

In contrast to these export gains from participation in trade in-
duced by reduction in industrial-country tariffs generally, the developing countries in general and Brazil in particular seem to have little to
gain from pressure for the maintenance of high industrial-country
tariffs designed to preserve a wider tariff preference margin. The
European and U.S. preference systems are currently hobbled by restrictions which in practice mean that at the margin extra exports
from many important LDCs do not enjoy free entry, and it is unlikely
that LDC export loss from erosion of preference margins would be
anywhere near the prospective export gains from broader and deeper
cuts of most-favored-nation (MFN) tariffs of industrial countries.[21]

Brazil could play a leadership role in the formation of LDC positions in the Tokyo Round. Perhaps an optimal strategy would be to
provide support for broader and deeper tariff cuts (generally favored
by the United States but less attractive to the Europeans, who wish
to maintain a significant tariff wall around the European Economic
Community, partly for reasons of political cohesion). This would be
preferable to pushing the alternative LDC position that opposes sizable
cuts in order to preserve preference margins. In return for this support, Brazil could ask the United States for commitments not to
extend "voluntary export controls" to other products vital to LDC
exports now and in the future.

New Economic Order. Brazil has already demonstrated a leadership
role in the monetary negotiations and may have the opportunity to
do so again in the trade negotiations. However, there is yet another
kind of negotiations likely to take place in the future in which
Brazil's role may be somewhat ambivalent: negotiations in UNCTAD
and other forums on a "new international economic order."

The striking success of the OPEC oil price rise has put "resource
diplomacy" muscle behind the demands of the developing countries
for revisions in the international economic system. The industrialized
countries must now take negotiations on proposals for a new order
more seriously than they have in the past.

Brazil appears to have two options in the forthcoming series of
negotiations on a "new order." One is to be a vocal champion of
across-the-board packages of proposals for favoring the developing
countries. The other is to take a pragmatic case-by-case approach to

---

[21] This same general conclusion is reached in Robert E. Baldwin and Tracy
Murray, "MFN Tariff Reductions and Developing Country Trade Benefits under
the GSP," *Economic Journal,* forthcoming.

various proposals, favoring the individual proposals most important for its own purposes. In addition Brazil could possibly act as a broker between the LDCs on the one hand and the industrial countries on the other, as U.S. policy makers appear to hope.[22]

It seems likely that Brazil will follow the course of pragmatic evaluation of individual issues, eschewing the option of highly visible advocacy of Third World causes. Other countries, even within Latin America, have already seized the rhetorical mantle of leadership of the LDCs on new economic order issues (Mexico with the Charter of Economic Rights and Duties, Venezuela with its oil strength). At the same time, many of the proposals likely to come out of these discussions will be primarily directed toward the very poorest countries, with marginal gains or perhaps even losses implied for countries at Brazil's economic level. Therefore Brazil in its own interest will be forced to be selective in supporting "new order" proposals.

Specific examples may illustrate this point. One of the proposals in the new order discussions is for generalized debt relief. Although Brazil's debt is high, future flows of private credit are extremely important to Brazil and those flows would be jeopardized by a highly vocal Brazilian campaign in favor of generalized concessional debt rescheduling. On the other hand, one likely proposal will be for the establishment of a package of commodities for inclusion in a buffer stock internationally financed, for the purpose of smoothing out price fluctuations. In the face of such a proposal Brazil may well find that upon evaluating the commodities involved and the proposed procedures, the proposal is in its favor.

There has already been an indication of the fact that Brazil intends to play a pragmatic role of case-by-case cooperation with the industrial countries: the mutual consultation agreement between the United States and Brazil in February 1976. As an example of an area of cooperation, Brazil appears to be eschewing participation in new producer cartels.[23] The implication is that Brazil is prepared to enter consumer-producer negotiations on commodity arrangements but does not intend to follow the alternative path of unilateral producer cartels—an alternative that, although usually considered in-

---

22 In the words of Secretary of State Kissinger: "They are playing a more significant role in the political councils of the world, not merely because of their enhanced economic strength but also because of their growing solidarity with the other developing countries of Africa and Asia. . . ." Statement before the House International Relations Committee, March 4, 1976 (Washington, D.C.: Bureau of Public Affairs, Office of Media Service), p. 1.

23 *Washington Post*, February 21, 1976, p. A9, and February 23, 1976, p. A23.

feasible for most products other than petroleum, continues to lurk in the background as the "threat from the third world." [24]

Another consideration may also lead Brazil to play a moderating role in commodity arrangements. Brazil imports certain key raw materials in addition to oil—among them, copper and wheat. To some extent Brazil's economy has characteristics similar to those of industrial countries relying on imported raw materials in at least some sectors. Any generalized resort to cartel pricing could injure Brazil in specific areas, perhaps by more than could be made up by resulting gains on prices of other commodities.

In sum, Brazil is most likely to play a pragmatic moderating role in the discussions on proposals for a new international economic order. Given Brazil's international economic weight, and in light of Brazil's already substantial role in the monetary reform negotiations, the country's part in the negotiations in the future will be important. And this fact appears to have been officially recognized by the recent mutual consultation agreement between Brazil and the United States.

Conclusion

Brazil stands at a turning point in its development strategy. After seven years of extraordinary success in expanding exports and raising the degree of openness in the Brazilian economy, the country faces very severe foreign sector constraints brought on by excessive import growth (especially in 1974) and mounting external debt. A new set of import controls, if permanent and growing, could mean the end of the outward-looking phase of Brazilian growth and a reversion to the import substitution strategy of the 1950s—despite the general recognition that import substitution industrialization has been milked dry. By contrast, with an international economy pulling out of recession, with appropriate exchange rate policy, and with an absence of new restrictions on industrial country import markets, it is possible and even likely that Brazil would be able to return to an export oriented strategy. (It would, however, be unrealistic to expect the high export growth rates of 1967-73 to repeat themselves, since their continuation would raise the openness of the economy to improbably high levels.)

As the largest single importer among the LDCs, one of the largest exporters, and the third largest LDC in population, Brazil occupies a

---

[24] C. Fred Bergsten, "The Threat from the Third World," *Foreign Policy*, no. 11 (Summer 1973).

position of natural economic leadership among the developing countries. It is most likely to exploit this position in the pursuit of limited pragmatic goals directly affecting its own economic interests, rather than in the advocacy of generalized measures for benefiting poor countries within a new economic order. A crucial area for Brazil is preventing further extension of non-tariff barriers to manufactured imports from developing countries, an objective Brazil can pursue through an active role in the Tokyo Round of trade negotiations. In the area of monetary reform Brazil has already played an important part in the development of workable revisions.

Overall, Brazil can play an important and responsible role in the evolution of the international economic system, occasionally acting as a broker between industrial and developing countries and, to the extent that it contributes to practical resolutions of problems, facilitating results favorable to both groups as well as to itself in particular.

4

TRENDS IN BRAZILIAN NATIONAL DEPENDENCY SINCE 1964

Robert A. Packenham

Is Brazilian dependence on the international environment greater than, less than, or the same as it was in 1964, when the current regime came to power? Observers of Brazilian affairs answer the question in varied ways. The prevailing view in Brazil, the United States, and Europe is that Brazil's dependence has increased. Indeed, Brazil since 1964 is seen as the prototype case of diluting or abandoning the quest for national autonomy in order to realize the (dubious) benefits of capitalist industrialization and development. Thus Ronald Chilcote characterizes Brazil's post-1964 relationship to the United States as a "subservient, dependent" one.[1] According to Marcio Moreira Alves the present Brazilian economy has become "totally dependent on foreign powers and their investments."[2] Helio Jaguaribe sees Brazilian dependency as "rising, and becoming increasingly irreversible."[3] He warns that unless these tendencies are corrected within certain

I am grateful to the Woodrow Wilson International Center for Scholars, the Center for Research in International Studies of Stanford University, and the Carnegie Endowment for International Peace for the grants for research and travel which made this study possible. I wish also to thank the director, Dr. Cleantho de Paiva Leite, and the staff of the Instituto Brasileiro de Relações Internacionais (IBRI) in Rio de Janeiro for office space and hospitality from August to December 1974. For especially valuable critical comments on an earlier draft of this paper I thank Fernando Henrique Cardoso, José Murilo de Carvalho, David Dye, Abraham Lowenthal, Thomas Skidmore, Carlos Eduardo Souza e Silva, and John Wirth. Responsibility for the final product is, of course, mine alone.

[1] Ronald L. Chilcote, book review of Frank D. McCann, *The Brazilian-American Alliance, 1937-1945* (Princeton, New Jersey: Princeton University Press, 1973), in *Annals of the American Academy of Political and Social Science*, no. 415 (September 1974), p. 232.

[2] Marcio Moreira Alves, *A Grain of Mustard Seed: The Awakening of the Brazilian Revolution* (Garden City, New York: Doubleday, Anchor, 1973), p. 162.

[3] Helio Jaguaribe, *Brasil: Crise e Alternativas* (Rio de Janeiro: Zahar, 1974), p. 72.

"historical deadlines" ranging from one to at most three decades hence, the chances of Brazil and other Latin American countries "ever obtaining an autonomous development will sharply decrease and will finally disappear altogether."[4] Examples of this point of view are legion. It is the conventional wisdom among intellectuals on at least three continents.

At the opposite end of the spectrum, some other analysts see Brazilian dependency to be waning and Brazil on the way toward great power status. Stefan Robock recently articulated this point of view in the following words:

> if Brazil can maintain its development drive, which has actually been underway for three decades, it will be one of the first major nations to cross the wide chasm separating the less developed and the developed countries. . . . It will become one of the major political powers of the world, as some observers are already forecasting.[5]

A British political scientist, the late Alastair Buchan, has also predicted eventual great power status for Brazil.[6] And the policy of the United States government toward Brazil, at least as expressed by the U.S. Department of State, is based on the same premise of Brazil's growing autonomy and eventual great power status—"it can't miss unless it goes the Argentine route."[7]

Are these writers and analysts all looking at the same country and the same period of time? They are—even though the enormous disparity in answers makes one wonder. Why do they differ so much?

A great part of the reason is that the notion of dependency is conceptualized in such an ambiguous way. It is a vague and sprawling concept which needs conceptual "sorting out" in order to be used empirically. In addition, much theorizing about dependency is merely tautological. Further, different analysts have different values and different views of the world which affect the way they perceive the Brazilian case. Still further, national dependency is an enormously complex and multifaceted phenomenon and different observers weigh the various elements differently in making estimates of overall national trends. These factors (and others) overlap and interact with

---

[4] Helio Jaguaribe, *Political Development: A General Theory and a Latin American Case Study* (New York: Harper and Row, 1973), p. 462.
[5] Stefan H. Robock, "Realizing the Miracle," *Saturday Review*, October 18, 1975, p. 30.
[6] Alastair Buchan, *The End of the Postwar Era: A New Balance of World Power* (London: Weidenfeld and Nicolson, 1974), pp. 58, 279.
[7] State Department official, talk at Stanford University, December 4, 1975.

one another: this helps to explain the variety of answers given to an ostensibly straightforward question.

The conceptual barriers to clear analysis of dependency may be even more serious than the data problems. Without conceptual clarity it is difficult to know how to interpret and present reliable data even when they do exist. Our main focus in this paper is empirical. For the most part the conceptual points we wish to make in it will flow from the organization, presentation, and analysis of information about the Brazilian case. However, given the importance of conceptual issues in dealing with dependency, a few words about these issues may be necessary at this point (and again in the conclusion of the paper).

(1) The concept of dependency is here defined in terms of power: that is, to be dependent is to be weak; to be autonomous (non-dependent) is to be strong.[8] Among other things, this definition allows the literature on power to teach us something about what dependency means, how it might be measured, and similar issues.

(2) Brazil, like all Latin American countries, is a dependent country, in the sense that compared to powerful countries like the United States or the Soviet Union it is relatively highly constrained by the international environment on most issues most of the time.

(3) Brazil, like all Latin American countries, is not totally helpless. Within the context of its dependence there is some room for maneuver. Indeed, in most respects, Brazil, by virtue of its size and power, is less constrained by the international environment than any other Latin American country.

(4) Dependency and its opposite (autonomy) can be defined as a continuous variable as well as a dichotomous variable. In other words, we can think of dependency not only in either/or terms (is Brazil dependent or autonomous?) but also in terms of degrees and trends (is Brazil more dependent than the United States? Is Brazil more or less dependent now than in 1964? Since dependence is defined in terms of power, this means that the question becomes, does Brazil have more or less power to guide its own destiny now than it did in 1964?).

---

[8] Of course, as indicated below no country is either totally dependent or totally autonomous. And there is a third category in the middle range—interdependence—for cases of mutual dependence within a context of overall parity of power. However, we emphatically reject the view that all countries are equally interdependent. These points are elaborated in my "Latin American Dependency Theories," in process. See also Joseph S. Nye, Jr., "Independence and Interdependence," Foreign Policy, no. 22 (Spring 1976), pp. 129-161.

(5) The aim of the present paper is to describe trends in the degree of dependency in one country over time, and in the process to clarify what is involved conceptually in such an undertaking. Describing *trends* is different from (although it overlaps with) describing *forms* or *types* of dependency; it is also different from *explaining* dependency—that is, identifying its causes.

(6) In this paper (and this is important) the notion of national dependency as such is separated analytically from the idea of exploitation and from the idea of inequality within the national unit. This separation is by no means intended to deny that exploitation or internal inequalities may accompany national dependency: surely they often do, but they need not. They are logically separable from dependency per se. In other words, exploitation and internal inequality may (or may not) be a consequence of dependency, but they should not be considered an aspect of the definition of dependency itself. At any rate, that is the way the matter is handled in this paper. (We will deal below with the empirical association between dependency and inequality in Brazil.)

(7) Finally, it is pertinent to say a word on the way this essay is related to the full range of concerns involved in the Latin American dependency paradigm as it is used to explain Latin American underdevelopment. This paradigm, which has gained great prominence in the last decade, employs a holistic approach which unites *by definition* the elements we have here separated analytically (national dependency, exploitation, internal inequality, capitalism, and so on) as well as a number of others.[9] The present essay focuses principally on just one of these elements, that is, national dependency. The decision to limit the inquiry in this essay to a description and analysis of national dependency over time is deliberate and considered, not inadvertent. In our view the holistic approach has serious conceptual problems that severely limit its utility as a guide to empirical research. We also find that there is plenty of substantive interest, complexity, and work merely in focusing on national dependency. Nevertheless, we recog-

---

[9] The most important contemporary dependency theorists are for the most part Latin Americans, but others have also written on the subject. Latin Americans include Fernando Henrique Cardoso, Theotonio dos Santos, Octávio Ianni, Helio Jaguaribe, Luciano Martins, Guillermo O'Donnell, Aníbal Quijano, José A. Silva Michelena, Osvaldo Sunkel, and Francisco Weffort. Contributors to the literature from outside Latin America include Susanne Bodenheimer, Frank Bonilla, James Cockcroft, André Gunder Frank, Johan Galtung, Dale Johnson, James Petras, Philippe Schmitter, A. W. and N. L. Singham, and Stanley and Barbara Stein. My comments about dependency writings are based on the works of these authors, as well as a few others. A detailed treatment of the dependency literature is given in my "Latin American Dependency Theories."

nize that others see it differently; it is therefore worth stating explicitly that this essay is not an exploration of the entire dependency framework or paradigm, but rather a description and analysis of one major and crucial aspect of it in the Brazilian case since 1964.

Bearing all this in mind, the purposes of this paper are two: first, to suggest answers to the substantive question raised at the outset about trends in Brazilian national dependency since 1964, and second, to address and (one hopes) to clarify some conceptual issues in the analysis of Latin American dependency that have relevance beyond the specific case.

We turn now to the Brazilian case. As indicated, to get anywhere in the analysis of dependency it is necessary to break the concept into various facets. Analysis of the theoretical literature on dependency and exposure to the realities of the Brazilian case since 1964 combine to suggest that there are five main facets in a useful description and analysis of Brazilian national dependency: (1) analysis of the total magnitude of national resources and productive capacity, (2) analysis of the degree of penetration of national resources and productive capacity by external lenders, investors, aid donors, and trade activity, (3) analysis of the qualitative nature of external penetration of national resources and productive capacity, (4) analysis of the skill and capacity of national leaders in using available resources and productive capacity to cope with the international environment, and (5) analysis of the degree to which developmental goals and values are nationally rather than externally determined.

The Magnitude of Brazilian Resources

All other things being equal, the more resources and productive capacity a nation has, the more power it has (the less dependent it is). Brazil, Mexico, and Argentina are less dependent than Panama because they have many more resources and productive capacity. That is to say, they are much more powerful than Panama on most issues most of the time. How does the Brazil of today compare with Brazil of 1964 in this facet of dependency?

Our answer to this question can be brief. By almost any conventional aggregate economic measure of the total magnitude of national resources and productive capacity, Brazil is less dependent today than it was in 1964. As is well known, Brazil's gross national product increased from 1968 through 1974 (inclusive) at an average rate of 10 percent per year: This rate of growth placed Brazil among the very fastest growing countries in the world. Whether one looks at gross national product, gross national product per capita, industrial output, manpower supply, total population, or nearly any other conventional measure of aggregate resource and production growth, Brazil's record during this period has been remarkable. Since the resources and production of most of the rest of the world were not growing nearly so fast, this record indicates a lessening of Brazil's dependence.

Of course, this says nothing about how the wealth was distributed internally during this period, whether the growth was optimal in the quality of life it produced for Brazilians, who controlled the use and benefits of these national resources, or about other questions which will be treated later. However, total magnitude of resources and productive capacity is unquestionably an essential facet of overall national dependency, and so far as it is concerned Brazil did very well indeed during the period since 1964.

External Penetration of Brazilian Resources

Both common sense and much of the theoretical literature on dependency suggest that it is one thing to have national resources and productive capacity located on national soil, while it is something else again to have these resources and capacities penetrated by external influences such as foreign investors, foreign lenders, foreign trade activities, and donors of foreign aid. In general, all other things being equal, the more a nation's economy is penetrated by loans, investments, aid, and reliance on external trade, the more dependent the nation is. To a significant degree the view that Brazil's overall dependence has increased since 1964 is based on the hypothesis that this particular facet of dependence has increased. Most of the evidence supports this hypothesis; some of it counters the hypothesis; and some of the evidence is incomplete or ambiguous.

In many significant ways external penetration of Brazil's economy has increased dramatically since 1964. The most dramatic indicator of this is the foreign debt. In the years 1960–64 the yearly average of the foreign debt was less than $3 billion. In 1972 the figure reached $10 billion. By the end of 1975 it was over $22 billion, and apparently still climbing.[10] Another indicator is foreign trade. The more foreign trade, the more reliance on the external economy—that is, the more external national dependence. In 1964 total exports

---

[10] *Boletim do Banco Central do Brasil*, various issues, as given in Werner Baer, "The Brazilian Growth and Development Experience, 1964-1975," Table 3, Chapter 2, this volume. See also William R. Cline, "Brazil's Emerging International Economic Role," Table 4, Chapter 3, this volume.

amounted to $1.43 billion; in 1974, they were $7.97 billion. In 1964, total imports were $1.09 billion; in 1972 they were $4.2 billion; in 1974, after a fourfold increase in the national oil bill and other increases, they were $12.5 billion.[11] Still another instrument of increased external economic penetration lies in multinational organizations like the World Bank and the International Monetary Fund. In general their impact on Brazil increased: it may be noted, for instance, Brazil replaced India as the recipient of the largest loans from the World Bank.

Foreign investment also increased dramatically. This trend was significantly more pronounced in portfolio investment (loans, finance capital) than in direct private investment (equity capital). Thus, net foreign loans to Brazil increased from a yearly average of $350 million in 1960–64 to a yearly average of $5.12 billion in 1972–74. Net foreign direct investment increased from a yearly average of $70 million in 1960–64 to a yearly average of $770 million in 1972–74.[12] This is an increase by a factor of nineteen in the annual amount of net foreign lending and an increase by a factor of eleven in the annual amount of net foreign direct investment during this period. Notice also that the absolute figures are much larger for loans than for direct investment.

Moreover, the increase in the foreign penetration of Brazil's economy according to the foregoing indicators has been significantly greater than the growth of the Brazilian economy as a whole. In 1964, Brazil's gross domestic product (GDP) was in the neighborhood of $21 billion, and per capita income about $270. By 1974, GDP was estimated to be about $56 billion and per capita GDP to be about $540. This means that gross domestic product increased roughly three times and per capita product increased roughly two times from 1964 to 1975.[13] As the figures given earlier indicate, however, the national debt increased about seven times during this same span of years, imports about eleven to twelve times, exports six to seven times, annual loans about nineteen times, and annual direct investment about eleven times. Or, to put the same point another way, if one takes

---

[11] Stefan H. Robock, *Brazil: A Study in Development Progress* (Lexington, Massachusetts: D. C. Heath and Company, 1975), p. 113. Robock uses Brazilian Central Bank sources. See also Baer, "The Brazilian Growth and Development Experience," Table 3, and Cline, "Brazil's Emerging International Role," Table 2.

[12] Baer, "The Brazilian Growth and Development Experience," Table 3, using Brazilian Central Bank sources.

[13] Calculated from Kenneth Ruddle and Kathleen Barrows, eds., *Statistical Abstract of Latin America* (Los Angeles: Latin American Center, University of California, January 1974), pp. 432-433, and Baer, "The Brazilian Growth and Development Experience," Table 1.

each of the foregoing indicators of external economic penetration of Brazil as a percentage of gross domestic product, first in 1964 and then in 1974, one finds that in each case the foreign share increased during the period. Thus, as a share of annual gross domestic product from 1964 to 1974, the foreign debt rose from 14 percent to 38 percent, imports from 5 percent to 21 percent, exports from 7 percent to 14 percent, annual foreign loans from 2 percent to 9 percent, and annual direct investment from 0.3 percent to 1.3 percent.[14]

All this indicates increased dependence for Brazil. There are a few relevant counter-trends, however. The most important relates to the role of the government in general and state enterprises in particular in the Brazilian economy. The quantitative role of the state in the Brazilian economy has been growing fairly steadily since 1930, including growth in the years since 1964. According to one informed estimate, the government sector accounted for over 60 percent of Brazil's fixed investment in 1969.[15] This trend did not subside in the 1970s, as the increasing debate over *estatização* ("statization") of the economy indicates. It is difficult to say whether this expansion in the state's role fully balances the increase in the role of the multinational corporations and in the importance of other foreign economic forces. It seems fairly clear, however, that it is a massive and dramatic expansion and counters that multinational and foreign increase to a considerable extent. (The big loser in this three-player game, it appears, is the Brazilian private sector. The private sector's loss is one reason for the present tactical marriage of convenience in Brazilian domestic politics between (1) domestic Brazilian capitalist entrepreneurs protesting both multinational corporations and Brazilian statism and (2) Brazilian socialists who oppose capitalist imperialism and the current Brazilian state. The entrepreneurs have even accused the regime of leftist tendencies; one article by J. C. de Macedo Soares Guimarães was published with the disarming title, "Communism and its new name: State Capitalism." Obviously the basis of the current alliance between such entrepreneurs and Brazilian socialists is not ideological.) [16]

---

[14] Calculated from sources given in notes 10-13 above.

[15] Werner Baer, Isaac Kerstenetzky, and Annibal V. Villela, "The Changing Role of the State in the Brazilian Economy," *World Development*, vol. 1, no. 11 (November 1973), pp. 30-31.

[16] The article by Macedo Soares Guimarães is in the *Jornal do Brasil*, August 1, 1975. I owe the reference to Alexandre de S. C. Barros, "The Changing Role of the State in Brazil: The Technocratic-Military Alliance," paper delivered at Sixth Annual Meeting of the Latin American Studies Association, Atlanta, Georgia, March 25-28, 1976. Barros makes the interesting argument that *estatizacão* is probably a bigger threat to foreign capital than to national capital.

Another counter-trend may be found in the area of bilateral aid from the United States. Brazil was a major recipient of U.S. economic and technical assistance in the immediate aftermath of the 1964 revolution. Since 1970, however, the flow of U.S. bilateral aid has slowed to a trickle, so that today it has practically no significance. From the point of view of U.S. economic influence on Brazil, the real action is in the private sector and the multilateral agencies.

Overall, the picture within this second facet of dependency is mixed. On balance, however, dependency here has almost certainly increased because of the weight of the first set of trends described. In contrast to the "closing" of the economy that characterized and accompanied growth through import substitution in the 1950s, Brazil's economy since 1964 has "opened up" and this means more dependence.

Qualitative Nature of External Penetration. Much of the argument that Brazil's dependency has increased has been based on qualitative structural features of the foreign penetration of Brazil's economy. According to this argument, even more important than total resources or total degree of foreign penetration is the qualitative nature of that penetration. In particular, according to this perspective, one needs to look at foreign penetration of the most dynamic sectors of the economy, that is, the sectors that are growing at the fastest rates. Thus, Moreira Alves argues that

> official figures, published to reassure Brazilians, state that only 6 percent of our national capital is foreign-owned. This already frightening percentage is misleading. . . . Six percent is an enormous amount of foreign dominance, especially if, as is the case, it is strategically placed in the most dynamic industries. Hitler's armies probably never controlled directly more than six percent of the economies of France, Poland, and the other occupied lands. This does not mean, however, that they could not master the total economic potential of these countries in order to strengthen Germany's war effort.[17]

Nearly all other writers on dependency, including the most sophisticated theorists, make a similar point, although usually without the overblown Hitlerian analogies. For instance, Fernando Henrique Cardoso argues that

---

[17] Moreira Alves, *A Grain of Mustard Seed*, pp. 163-164.

in Brazil the level of foreign private investment in the dynamic industrial sectors has been so high and so sustained that the state sector and national entrepreneurs clearly no longer play a dominant role in such key decision-making centers as the capital goods and durable consumer goods industries.[18]

Clearly the qualitative nature of external penetration is an important aspect of dependency. Moreover, dependency theorists are correct in general in their contention that some if not most of the particularly dynamic sectors of the economy have been penetrated disproportionately (that is, more than in the economy overall) by foreign actors and influences. However, the qualitative nature of external penetration has several aspects, not all of which—in the Brazilian case—indicate increasing dependency. In fact, if one considers a wide array of qualitative features of external penetration and domestic control, there is a strong case that Brazil's overall dependence qualitatively has decreased rather than increased since 1964.

It is quite true that some of the most dynamic sectors have been disproportionately penetrated by foreign capital. Among these sectors are trucks and automobiles, tractors, industrial machinery, pharmaceuticals, tobacco, office machinery, rubber products, perfume, and plastics.[19] (All of these sectors are foreign-dominated; most but not necessarily all of them have been dynamic.) It is not true that all the most dynamic sectors have been highly penetrated: shoes, sugar and soybeans are among the particularly dynamic sectors where domestic control has been high. Nor are all the sectors where foreign control is high necessarily dynamic; Morley and Smith calculate that "about 60 percent of foreign investment profits come from the nondynamic or vegetative part of manufacturing." [20] Even so, the argument that

---

[18] Fernando Henrique Cardoso, "Associated-Dependent Development: Theoretical and Practical Implications," in Alfred Stepan, ed., *Authoritarian Brazil: Origins, Policies, and Future* (New Haven and London: Yale University Press, 1973), p. 144.

[19] Robock, *Brazil: A Study in Development Process*, pp. 61-65; Baer, "The Brazilian Growth and Development Experience," Table 2. On foreign control of various sectors see also Richard S. Newfarmer and William F. Mueller, *Multinational Corporations in Brazil and Mexico: Structural Sources of Economic and Noneconomic Power*, Report to the Subcommittee on Multinational Corporations of the Committee on Foreign Relations, U.S. Senate (Washington, D.C.: U.S. Government Printing Office, August 1975), pp. 112-113; and the study by IPEA (Instituto de Planejamento Econômico e Social), "Multinational Corporations," as reported in the *Jornal do Brasil*, September 15, 1974, p. 28.

[20] Samuel A. Morley and Gordon W. Smith, "The Effect of Changes in the Distribution of Income on Labor, Foreign Investment, and Growth in Brazil," in Stepan, ed., *Authoritarian Brazil*, pp. 136-137.

foreign capital—especially new foreign capital—is concentrated in the faster growing sectors of the economy appears to be largely correct.[21]

There are, however, other aspects of foreign penetration besides the degree of penetration in the particularly dynamic sectors. One qualitative consideration is, how diversified is the Brazilian economy? How diversified are Brazil's trade partners and sources of loans, investment, aid, and technology? In particular, has this diversification increased or decreased since 1964? In general, all other things being equal, the greater the diversification, for any level of aggregate penetration, the less will be Brazil's dependency, since more diversification gives Brazil more options and less dependence on any one sector, partner, or source of capital.

According to virtually every one of the indicators of diversification just cited, Brazil seems to be less dependent today than it was in 1964. There has been a definite and very strong trend toward diversification in sources of foreign investment in Brazil during this period. The United States remains the largest single foreign investor in Brazil, but its share in total external investment is down from a high of nearly 50 percent of total foreign investment in the middle and late 1960s to 34 percent in 1974. Between 1969 and 1973 France, Japan, Switzerland, the United Kingdom, West Germany, and Canada all expanded their investments in Brazil at a faster rate than the United States.[22] To some extent this diversification in sources of foreign investment in Brazil may be offset by the coordination that occurs through multinational enterprises. To the extent such transnational coordination occurs, the diversification of the sources of foreign investment may not have any real meaning. This is an issue that deserves further study. Still, it is impossible to believe that this diversification is entirely meaningless.

Similar trends toward increasing diversification are evident on nearly every other indicator of external economic penetration. For example, Brazil's commodity export structure has diversified markedly. Coffee constituted 42 percent of total exports during the period from 1965 through 1969 but only 12.6 percent in 1974. During this period,

[21] One of the many important research needs in this area is to distinguish portfolio capital from equity capital in the dynamic sectors. It is a reasonable, but as yet unresearched, hypothesis that equity capital (that is, direct investment) tends to be found in less dynamic sectors than portfolio investments (that is, loans). A related hypothesis, about "old" and "new" foreign investment sectors, is advanced by Morley and Smith, "The Effect of Changes in the Distribution of Income," p. 137.

[22] *Jornal do Brasil*, September 19, 1974, p. 29 (using Brazilian Central Bank sources). The same material appears in Robock, *Brazil*, p. 67, and in the *Boletim do Banco Central do Brasil*, May 1975.

however, manufactures increased from 7.2 to 27.7 percent, and sugar from 5.0 to 15.8 percent. Soybeans did not exist as part of the export structure in 1965–69 but represented 7.4 percent of it in 1974. Other commodities that did not exist in the export structure in 1965–69 constituted an impressive 28.4 percent in 1974.[23]

Brazil's list of trading partners has also been diversified. The United States share of Brazilian trade in 1967–68 was 33.2 percent; in 1974, it was only 21.5 percent. The only countries besides the United States whose share of Brazilian trade was less in 1974 than in 1967–68 were the seven countries of the Soviet bloc, whose share fell from 6.2 to 4.1 percent, and the five countries now in the European Free Trade Area, where the proportion dropped from 5.3 to 3.7 percent. During this same span of time, however, the share of the European Community (nine countries) increased from 32.6 to 34.2 percent, that of the Latin American Free Trade Area (ten countries including the Andean bloc) from 9.8 to 11.9 percent, Japan from 3.3 to 5.7 percent, and Asia (excluding Japan), Oceania, Spain, Africa, the Middle East, and the rest of the world, from 14.9 to 18.9 percent.[24] Brazil's internal economy has certainly diversified. Foreign sources of loans and technology have also diversified during this period. Again, the significance of all these trends is only partly reduced through the effects of transnational coordination by the multinationals.

For a long time it has been argued, and properly so, that Brazil's heavy reliance on one country (the United Kingdom or the United States), or one commodity (sugar or coffee, for example) restricted its options and made it highly dependent on the international environment. It follows, of course, that diversification in sources of capital, export structure, trade partners, technology, and internal economic activities reduces Brazil's dependence. And that is what has happened since 1964.

A third qualitative aspect of foreign penetration, besides the degree of penetration in the dynamic sectors and diversification of partners and sources, is the question of foreign penetration of the most vital sectors of the national economy. By *most vital sectors* I mean not the sectors that are necessarily the fastest growing, but rather those sectors that are most crucial (1) for the economic infrastructure of the country (sectors that are bases for the rest of the economy to grow and function), and (2) for the national security of Brazil militarily, strategically, diplomatically, and economically. The

---

[23] Baer, "The Brazilian Growth and Development Experience," Table 5.
[24] *Boletim do Banco Central do Brasil*, December 1974, pp. 144-151, and March 1975, p. 193, as cited in Robock, *Brazil*, p. 115.

more these vital sectors are penetrated by foreign actors, the more dependent Brazil will be; the less they are penetrated, the less dependent Brazil will be. What is the trend since 1964?

It appears that the trend is overwhelmingly toward greater Brazilian control of the economy's most vital sectors. The major agent of this increasing national control is, of course, the Brazilian state. Since 1964, continuing a secular trend that began at least as far back as 1930 (and arguably as far back as the middle of the nineteenth century), the Brazilian national state has taken increasing control over vital national economic sectors. It is now the principal controlling agent in the following industries and sectors: oil, steel, electric power generation, railroads, ocean transport, harbors, banking, iron ore, telecommunications, atomic energy, and highways. In addition, the state has powerful fiscal and monetary tools through its control of the Central Bank, the Bank of Brazil, the National Development Bank, the National Housing Bank, and the National Price Control Council (CIP).[25] Each of these sectors and industries, including banking, is vital to national security and the economic vitality of the country. If they are not all more vital than trucks, automobiles, and capital goods, most of them are much more significant than pharmaceuticals and light manufacturing, where foreign capital is controlling.

One other area that must be mentioned in this context (the quality of foreign penetration) is technology dependency. Brazil's dependence on foreign technology is massive. I have heard it estimated that 97 percent of Brazil's productive capacity in the industrial sectors is dependent on foreign technology.[26] Whatever the correct figures may be—and so far as I know systematic data on the subject are lacking—it seems clear, judging from the estimates of informed Brazilians, that the absolute level of technology dependence is extremely high. However, our question here is not the absolute level but the trend since 1964, and in this context we would note two points. First, the sources of technology, like other economic resources, have diversified in this period. Second, since the level of dependence in 1964 was so high, it could not possibly increase very much, and small steps have been taken since then to find ways to reduce technological dependence. Both these moves, however, appear to be in very early stages.[27] Hence, while the trend in this facet is toward slightly less dependence,

[25] Baer, Kerstenetzky, and Villela, "The Changing Role of the State in the Brazilian Economy," pp. 23-24.

[26] Interviews in Brazil, August to December 1974.

[27] Baer, Kerstenetzky, and Villela, "The Changing Role of the State in the Brazilian Economy," p. 30.

the magnitude of the change is not yet great enough to have much meaning.

Summing up on this third facet (qualitative nature of external penetration), we can say that since 1964 Brazil's dependence has increased significantly in the particularly dynamic sectors, decreased significantly in the most vital sectors, decreased marginally in technology dependency, and decreased significantly in diversification. These are mixed results, but there are more indicators indicating a decrease in dependency than indicating an increase, and—in my view—control over oil, steel, electric power, transportation, and so on, are more crucial for Brazilian autonomy than control over the other sectors. But different observers weigh these different dimensions differently. According to Moreira Alves, for instance, "The state occupies barren unprofitable economic space, as in the case of the railroads we bought back from the British, or that of the steel industry, which demands heavy investments for mediocre profits." According to him, what really matters is "everything that we consume in our daily lives" such as Coca-Cola, toothpaste, and aspirin.[28]

Skill and Capacity of National Leadership

The foregoing three facets of dependency comprise the magnitude, control, and structure of national resources and productive capacity. Now we turn to the ends for which these resources and capacities are used and the skill and capacity of the leaders to use them. Let us consider first the question of the skill and capacity of national leaders. Ceteris paribus (as always), the more skillful the leaders are in using the resources they have to work with, the less dependent is the country. What has been the trend since 1964?

The variables here are "softer" than those used earlier, and data are more scarce. Still, some observations can be made. The skill of Brazilian leaders, especially in the government, in dealing with the international business community seems to have improved markedly.[29] Brazilians and foreigners alike report that Brazilian government officials and businessmen have tended to drive harder bargains in inter-

---

[28] Moreira Alves, A Grain of Mustard Seed, pp. 164-165.

[29] The statements in this paragraph are based primarily on interviews and observations in Washington, D.C. from September 1973 to August 1974, and in various parts of Brazil, mainly Rio de Janeiro and Brasília, from August to December 1974. They are also documented in Newfarmer and Mueller, Multinational Corporations in Brazil and Mexico, pp. 99-101; Baer, Kerstenetzky, and Villela, "The Changing Role of the State in the Brazilian Economy," p. 30; and Robock, Brazil, pp. 66, 68.

national economic negotiations since 1964 than during most of the years before 1964. The terms of joint ventures involving foreigners have stiffened to Brazil's benefit. During the period that the Brazilian government was pushing exports as a leading sector in the economic boom, foreign firms were told to export whether they wanted to or not. Brazil pays strict and close attention to agreements on patents, licenses, and royalty payments for foreign technology, and it enforces these agreements. The provisions have been tightened and royalty payments have been reduced. Laws on remittance of profits are looser than those prevailing in the period 1961–64 (which was very tight indeed) but tighter than the legislation on the books between 1953 and 1961. Brazilian diplomats have further enhanced their reputation as the most able corps in Latin America.

The expansion in the size of the Brazilian state has given it greater capacity to cope with the international and national environments. The economic boom has made Brazil more attractive to foreign investors and lenders and thus enabled Brazilians to drive harder bargains. Brazil since 1964 has had a government of military men delegating power to technocrats, who have on the whole been more skilled in governing roles than were their predecessors. For instance, the level of competence and sophistication in economic discourse has increased significantly with the marked increase in the pool of trained economists and other technocrats since 1964. (Whether one views this as good or bad depends, of course, on one's view of the value of sophistication in economic discourse. Whichever way one comes out on that question, however, one must still agree that the degree of skill in using resources for the ends chosen by the government has increased.)

As must be obvious from the earlier discussion of the expanding role of multinational corporations in Brazil, the post-1964 regime has encouraged much more foreign economic involvement in Brazil than the Goulart government. The question here is not the amount of foreign penetration but the terms on which that penetration has been negotiated and the overall skill of the Brazilian government and private leaders in managing Brazil's resources. When we compare Brazil before and after 1964, the trend seems pretty clearly to be up.

The Degree to Which Developmental Goals and Values are Nationally Determined. The fifth and final facet we wish to consider here is the degree to which developmental goals and values are shaped by national or extranational forces. In other words, what are the developmental uses to which Brazil's resources and productive capacity are put, and are these objectives nationally or externally determined? The less Brazil's developmental model reflects national rather than extranational priorities, the more dependent is the country.

The main features of the Brazilian developmental model since 1964 are well known: very high rates of growth in aggregate terms; a reliance on the market and on material incentives with substantial governmental intervention in key areas; increasing class, regional, and urban-rural social and economic inequalities; political authoritarianism and repression; and so on. One can elaborate the features at great length and argue about details, but the broad outlines are clear and require no further discussion here.[30]

For our purposes the significant question is the degree to which this developmental model is a product of internal or external causes. The prevailing view is that the role of external variables in shaping the developmental model has increased since 1964. Those who see Brazil as the prototype of dependent capitalist development argue their case on many grounds, including the considerations reviewed above; but no part of their argument is given greater weight by them than this fifth consideration. I should say, however, that while there may be something to be said for this position, there is more to be said on the other side. If one applies this fifth criterion systematically and rigorously it is clear that the Brazilian developmental model is less shaped by external considerations today than it was in 1964.

(I should also say here, as a brief aside, that writers on dependency sometimes treat the features of the Brazilian model as themselves indicators of dependency. But this is to abandon national constraints as the definition of national dependency and to replace them with other definitions and criteria. When this is done dependency means "the capitalist model," and its opposite, autonomy, is defined as "the socialist model." There is, I believe, a case to be made for this approach, and also a case against it. Whatever the merits and demerits of this intellectual strategy, it is different from the one being employed in this paper.

(It is important to note that the strategy I am using in this paper *is used* by dependency theorists. Nearly all of them define dependency in terms of national constraint. The trouble is that most of them also use the second strategy just mentioned *in the same piece of writing.* This mixing of definitions and intellectual strategies is a serious intellectual problem in the vast majority of dependency writings,[31] and it is

---

[30] For details, see Robert A. Packenham, "Yankee Impressions and Brazilian Realities," *The Wilson Quarterly,* vol. 1, no. 1 (October 1976).

[31] See note 9 above and the text accompanying it.

one major reason I have chosen to select just one of the two potentially conflicting definitions that the theorists use and to stick to it rather than oscillating back and forth between different definitions as they frequently do.)

Returning now to our main theme, the first set of reasons for doubting the prevailing orthodoxy on the fifth facet of dependency relates to the *direction* of changes in Brazil since 1964. Are these changes more toward a model of development that is *foreign*, or are they affirmations and reaffirmations, for good or for ill, of profoundly *national* impulses? Clearly they are much more the latter than the former.

Let us start with economic aspects of the model, where the prevailing view seems to find its strongest support. It is true that this economic model is essentially capitalist. But this is hardly outside the tradition of Brazilian nationalism: Brazilian institutions have long been essentially capitalist. Moreover, within that historical experience there has long been a tendency toward significant state involvement in economic matters; the post-1964 regime has maintained and indeed expanded upon those tendencies. The Goulart government (1961–64) was anything but socialist. What passed for moves in a socialist direction in the Goulart years were, with a few exceptions, mainly a combination of rhetoric, hypocrisy, adventurism, and incompetence. Few if any governments before 1961 were any less capitalist or more socialist than the present regime; they were just less effective. So it is hard, even when we look at the economic model, to make a strong case that external influence increased significantly after 1964.

Consider the political aspects of the model. Those who argue that the present authoritarianism and repression reflect increased foreign influence assume that such elements of liberal constitutional democracy as existed from 1946 to 1964 reflected the great national tradition of Brazil more than they reflected foreign influences, and that this tradition was thwarted by the coup in 1964. This assumption is dubious. The "great tradition" in Brazilian politics is neither liberal nor radical (although it contains significant elements of the former and minor elements of the latter) but patriarchal, patrimonial, hierarchical, paternalistic, clientelistic, and corporatist (or, in Alfred Stepan's recent phrase, "organic-statist").[32] It is much more plausible

---

[32] For extensive analyses of these themes see the classic works of such Brazilian writers as Azevedo Amaral, Sergio Buarque de Holanda, Gilberto Freyre, Raymundo Faoro, Victor Nunes Leal, and Oliveira Vianna. A number of younger Bazilian social scientists, including Alexandre de Souza Barros, José Murilo de Carvalho, Wanderley Guilherme dos Santos, Bolivar Lamounier, Fabio Wanderley Reis, and Simon Schwartzman, have begun to deepen our understanding of these

to perceive what has happened since 1964 as a reaffirmation in contemporary terms of authentically Brazilian political models than as an indication of expanded foreign influence, although obviously both internal and external elements were present. The United States supported the coup and, in general, has supported the post-1964 regime. This by itself, however, does not necessarily mean the political model reflected expanded foreign influence.

By now the thrust of my argument ought to be clear. It finds its strongest support in respect of the social model. In 1964 social and economic inequalities in Brazil were already among the highest in the world. Since 1964 they have widened still further. This is perhaps the most disturbing feature in the entire developmental model: the existence of political repression is abhorrent but affects *directly* only a very small proportion of the population while the social problems affect the vast majority of the population.

And what feature could be more Brazilian than socioeconomic inequality? Where are the egalitarian elements in the Brazilian tradition that are being smothered by foreign pressures? Where in the external environment is there anything to compare with the elitism, the tolerance for massive socioeconomic disparities, and the preference for social harmony and abhorrence of profound social conflicts that are unquestioned assumptions in Brazil's national tradition?

Those who contend that increasing inequalities in Brazil reflect increasing foreign influence on the developmental model also say that most of this external influence comes from the United States. In this view—which is surely the new conventional wisdom in academic circles in the United States and which is an unchallenged article of faith among many Brazilian and Latin American intellectuals—the impact of the United States on Brazil's social model since 1964 is seen to be mainly or exclusively anti-egalitarian.

It is of course true and important that capitalism requires and generates socioeconomic inequalities; that U.S. cold war anti-communism has opposed radical revolutionary movements; and that liberal U.S. developmentalism favors incrementalism and tends to abhor

---

traditional structures and processes and their contemporary manifestations. Useful discussions in English include Douglas A. Chalmers, "Political Groups and Authority in Brazil," in Riordan Roett, ed., *Brazil in the Sixties* (Nashville, Tennessee: Vanderbilt University Press, 1972), pp. 51-76; Riordan Roett, *Brazil: Politics in a Patrimonial Society* (Boston: Allyn and Bacon, 1972); Philippe Schmitter, *Interest Conflict and Political Change in Brazil* (Stanford, California: Stanford University Press, 1971); Alfred Stepan, *The State and Society* (Princeton: Princeton University Press, forthcoming).

genuine social revolution.[33] But the overwhelming thrust of the great traditions of Brazilian nationalism has always been at least as anti-Communist and anti-radical as the thrust of U.S. policy and much *more* socially elitist.

Where in the North American tradition, for example, is there anything to compare with the landlord in Brazil's Northeast who told his tenants who wanted to organize a peasant league:

> Everything has been ordained by God. He knows what He is doing. If He gives land to me and not to you, to reject this is to rebel against God. Such a rebellion is a mortal sin. . . . You have to accept poverty on earth in order to gain eternal life in heaven. The poor live in God's grace. The rich don't. In this way you are more fortunate than I, since you are closer to heaven.[34]

Not even the most conservative Republican or southern Democrat in the United States would support this philosophy. Very few U.S. citizens, to take another example, are familiar or comfortable with the social distinctions and hierarchies involved in relationships with *empregadas domésticas, porteiros,* and *babás* (domestic servants, doormen, and nannies) which all Brazilians (including the most radical ones) have known all their lives, take entirely for granted, and rarely see as the contradictions to liberal or radical ideological principles that they manifestly are.

American liberal doctrines and practices are conservative when compared to radical doctrines and practices, but they are progressive when compared to social conservatism. And Brazil's national tradition is one of the most conservative in Latin America and without question far more conservative than North America's. The liberal-conservative distinction has understandably—and perhaps properly—been neglected in the recent period of disenchantment with liberalism,

---

[33] The first point is true by definition. However, the degree of social and economic inequality varies enormously among capitalist societies. And whether or not capitalist economic growth, in societies like Brazil that are already highly inegalitarian, requires increasing those inequalities, is an extremely debatable question. An excellent review of the literature on this issue is William R. Cline, "Distribution and Development: A Survey of the Literature," *Journal of Development Economics,* vol. 1 (1975), pp. 359-400.

The second and third points are documented, among other places, in Joseph A. Page, *The Revolution that Never Was: Northeast Brazil, 1955-1964* (New York, N.Y.: Grossman Publishers, 1972); Riordan Roett, *The Politics of Foreign Aid in the Brazilian Northeast* (Nashville, Tennessee: Vanderbilt University Press, 1972); Robert A. Packenham, *Liberal America and the Third World: Political Development Ideas in Foreign Aid and Social Science* (Princeton, New Jersey: Princeton University Press, 1973).

[34] Quoted in Page, *The Revolution that Never Was,* p. 43.

but it has not disappeared, remains significant, deserves more attention than it receives, and severely weakens the prevailing argument.

It would seem that the case is very strong for the view that changes in Brazil's developmental model have tended to reaffirm rather than counter authentic Brazilian traditions. To make the opposite case is to make a counterfactual argument. It is to recognize that Brazil's national traditions are capitalist, authoritarian, and elitist, but to argue that these traditions *would have changed* in a socialist, democratic, egalitarian direction were it not for the coup/Revolution of 1964, which was supported by the United States. On some such grounds as these one might argue that the effect of the external environment on Brazil's development model since 1964 has increased rather than decreased.

Without question this is an analytic possibility. It is the implicit or explicit argument of many writers. The substantive merit of this line of reasoning is highly debatable, of course, and in our view extremely dubious. Our interpretation rests on the record of Brazil's history for nearly five centuries. Our approach stresses what has happened; it pays less attention to what might have happened, especially if it is extremely different from what had happened in the past. It does not invent a history that has not occurred. Counterfactual history, by contrast, underplays what has happened and emphasizes what might have happened. It requires the invention of a history that has never occurred. Nevertheless, each approach has its strengths and weaknesses; the reader will have to take his pick and assess the argument that is constructed on each approach.

So far our reasons for doubting that foreign influences on the developmental model have increased since 1964 have been reasons related to the directions of changes in the model. We have been noticing that the changes have tended to reaffirm rather than counter authentic Brazilian national traditions. We now turn to changes in the magnitude of Brazil's capacity for setting its own developmental course.

Our argument here has only two parts and can be stated briefly. First, the logic of the earlier part of our analysis leads toward the conclusion that foreign influences on the model have declined rather than increased. That is, insofar as Brazil's overall power position in the world has increased, its capacity to steer its own course internally has also increased. Second, Brazil's capacity to steer its own developmental course has increased because the earlier secular trend toward expanding Brazilian nationalism (a trend beginning at least by 1930) has continued unabated during the post-1964 period.

This latter fact is not sufficiently appreciated. It is frequently argued that the receptivity of the post-1964 regime to foreign capital, its agreement on many fundamental issues with major capitalist powers, and various other factors imply a decrease or abandonment of Brazilian nationalism. *None of the several myths about contemporary Brazil is more pervasive or more fundamentally in error than this one.* The strategy, tactics, and style of current Brazilian nationalism differ significantly from pre-1964 strategy, tactics, and style, but no one can doubt that the trend continues.

Consider, for example, the incidence of major diplomatic conflicts and their outcomes. Although U.S.-Brazilian diplomatic relations have been mostly positive since 1964, there has been an increasing number of points of tension and conflict on which Brazil has prevailed during this period. Among these have been the two-hundred mile limit, population-control diplomacy in Stockholm, Brazil's pro-Arab policy in general and its anti-Zionism vote in the United Nations in particular, Brazil's support for the MPLA in Angola, and, perhaps most significantly, the Brazil-West Germany accord on nuclear reactors.[35] By any reasonable standard these are central issues of foreign policy, not marginal ones. They show an intensification of Brazilian nationalism and a decline in Brazilian dependence. The following statement by the late J. A. de Araújo Castro, a career diplomat who for many years was Brazil's ambassador in Washington, illustrates the kind of ideology that lies behind these diplomatic maneuvers, and indeed behind the entire posture of the post-1964 regime toward the international environment:

> No country can escape its destiny and, fortunately, or unfortunately, Brazil is condemned to greatness. . . . Small, mediocre solutions are neither appropriate nor interesting to Brazil. . . . We have to think big and plan on a grand scale. . . . In a word: the primordial objective of the Foreign Policy of Brazil is the neutralization of all external factors which might limit its National Power. This policy could be neither more authentic nor more Brazilian. Nationalism is not, for us, an attitude of isolation, of prevention, or of hostility. It is, on the contrary, a strong impulse toward international participation.[36]

[35] Norman Gall, "Atoms for Brazil, Dangers for All," *Foreign Policy,* no. 23 (Summer 1976), pp. 155-201; Eul-Soo Pang, "Brazil's Pragmatic Nationalism," *Current History,* vol. 68, no. 401 (January 1975), pp. 5-10, 38.

[36] J. A. de Araújo Castro, "O Congelamento do Poder Mundial," *Revista Brasileira de Estudos Políticos,* no. 33 (January 1972), p. 30.

As this statement makes clear, the aim of Brazilian international cooperation and participation is not to abandon Brazilian nationalism but to enhance it. Brazil's present leaders aim to play the international game and to come out ahead. Their course (like every other course) is risky and uncertain, and they could fail. Moreover, one may count the developmental model they have chosen as gravely flawed. But that is a different issue. Brazilian nationalism has not declined since 1964, and this fact is another reason to doubt the claim of expanding foreign control over the developmental model.

In sum: in the fifth facet of dependency, Brazil is less, not more, dependent on the international environment now than it was in 1964.

Summary and Conclusions

Summing up this survey of trends in Brazilian dependency since 1964, we may set our findings in tabular form:

Facet of Dependency	*Trend since 1964*
Total magnitude of resources and productive capacity	*Less* dependency
Degree of external penetration	Mixed; in general *more* dependency
Quality (structural features) of external penetration	Mixed; in general *less* dependency
Leaders' skill in using resources and productive capacity	*Less* dependency
Degree of external influence over developmental model	*Less* dependency

This analysis indicates that Brazil is clearly less dependent in three of the five facets, generally less dependent in one, and generally more dependent in one. These findings are much more uniform than was expected when the inquiry was begun. The biggest surprises were on the third and fifth facets of dependency. Much of the prevailing view has rested on the argument that trends in these areas were toward greater dependency. However, on these two, as on two others, if one truly applies the criteria advanced by writers on dependency, then the trends are clearly toward less rather than more national dependency.

Our analysis has concentrated on economic facets because they are intrinsically important and because they are the core of the argument of writers on dependency. It is possible to explore other facets besides those examined here. For instance, one could explore more than we have the incidence of diplomatic conflicts and their outcomes. (Our brief examination indicated a strong trend toward less dependence.) One might also explore military and cultural aspects of dependency. It would be interesting to see how trends in these areas would compare to the trends identified in this paper.

Another topic we did not examine in detail is the oil crisis and its impact on Brazilian dependence. Without altering any of our previous and subsequent conclusions, we would like to make a stipulation about oil. Brazil imports about 75 percent of its oil, most of it crude oil whose refining takes place in Brazil. Although Brazil's oil suppliers have diversified since 1964, rising oil costs since 1973 have significantly hurt the Brazilian economy. However, this factor has affected almost the entire world—not just Brazil. Of course, Brazil has been more damaged by the oil crisis than the Arabs and the other producers, the United States, the Soviet Union, China, and perhaps a few other countries; but it has been less drastically affected than the fourth world, many other Third World countries, and even a number of industrialized nations (such as the United Kingdom, Japan, Italy). Moreover, the source of Brazil's difficulties regarding oil is not, of course, the industrialized center; it is other parts of the "dependent" periphery, namely, the OPEC countries. The stipulation, therefore, is that for purposes of the present inquiry oil is better considered a constant than a variable affecting the degree of Brazilian dependency. (This stipulation will be acceptable to dependency writers, who have said little about the oil crisis. Indeed, for most of them the oil crisis cannot have happened because the Arab states, Iran, Venezuela, Ecuador, Nigeria, and other members of the oil cartel are part of the dependent—helpless—periphery.)

Before stating some overall conclusions that might be drawn from our analysis, let us note some inferences and conclusions that should not be drawn from it. First, and most important, we emphasize that a definitive answer to the question posed at the beginning of this essay is impossible, even after our analyses. Even though dependency has diminished according to four of the five indicators we have used, it is not possible to say definitively that overall national dependency has declined. Not only are the data themselves always open to correction; more important, other analysts might use slightly different criteria, and there is always the problem of what weight to give to the various facets of national dependency.

The weighting issue is most important here. We have seen that for a given historical span of time dependency can go up according to one indicator and down according to another indicator. How can one aggregate these contrasting trends into an overall judgment? The question is not an easy one. For some observers the increase in external economic penetration might outweigh all the other trends. Others might give greater weight to the four facets where dependency has declined, and therefore come to the judgment that "in general" national dependency has decreased. (For the latter group the task would be more difficult if the results were more mixed—say, for example, up in two areas, down in two others, and mixed in the fifth.) Each set of observers has a reasonable view, and there is no strictly scientific and objective way to resolve the differences between them. The weights assigned to the various factors reflect values, general theoretical perspectives, and views of the world, as well as reflecting social science considerations more narrowly defined.

This problem of weights is inherent in complex multifaceted concepts like national dependency. There is no way to avoid it except to abandon the concepts, and that is neither realistic nor desirable. As long as one needs to use macroconcepts, it is better to be explicit and as rigorous as possible than to ignore problems of definition, weights, and so on as if they did not exist. In this way one can at least partly separate questions of logic, fact, and inference from questions of perspective, values, and ideology. And that is one of the main objectives of social science.

A second caveat is that we have not tried to write about the future. In this paper we have indicated some trends from 1964 to 1975 on a number of facets of Brazilian national dependency that have been discussed in the literature. We have not tried to indicate whether these trends will continue, increase, or decline in the future. To do this would require a much longer paper—and, among other things, a theory or set of theories about national dependency—that we do not choose to try just now. Our aim has been to describe some historical trends and to use and refine some concepts. This we hope and believe we have done. We have not tried to predict the future.

A third and final caveat is, as we noted at the beginning of the paper, that the foregoing analysis does not address all the features of the entire dependency paradigm all at once. We have limited our inquiry to the problem of national dependence. We have not included detailed investigation into such themes as the nature of Brazilian authoritarianism, social inequalities, or Brazil's economic institutions. To be sure, we have touched on these themes, especially in our discussion of the degree to which the Brazilian developmental model is shaped by the external environment. But we have not given the same amount of attention to these questions as to the question of national dependency.

The reasons for our focus here are essentially two. First, as a conceptual matter we think it is essential to distinguish national dependence analytically from a series of other complexes of variables which in the dependency paradigm are united by definition. Second, we believe that national dependency is, to put it mildly, already an enormously rich, fascinating, multifaceted analytic theme providing more than enough work for the energetic social scientist. It is also a topic of vital importance from many different theoretical and policy perspectives—including, of course, the perspective of the dependency paradigm. Thus there is no need to deal simultaneously with all the other themes that dependency writers deal with in order to make a consideration of the topic interesting and valuable.

Our approach does *not*, moreover, reduce the focus to a single one-dimensional phenomenon that ignores the ambiguity, variety, and contradictions that pervade real social processes. Indeed, as we have seen repeatedly, national dependency itself is multifaceted and contradictory; it can and does go up in one aspect and down in another. Our view is that any set of phenomena as rich and complicated as this one deserves, *indeed requires*, detailed and systematic analysis in its own right. Such analysis need not be always accompanied by a complementary treatment of all the other themes embedded in the dependency paradigm. For many purposes it is better to concentrate one's efforts.

So much for cautions and caveats. In a more positive vein, the most important substantive conclusion of this essay is to challenge the prevailing view that Brazilian national dependency has increased since 1964. The analysis we have carried out calls that view sharply into question. This conclusion is in a sense the other side of the cautionary point we made earlier. If it is risky to conclude from our analysis that national dependency has declined overall, it is also dangerous to contend that national dependency has increased. The weighting problem and other issues apply just as much to one hypothesis as to the other. What the foregoing analysis can and does teach us is that the conventional wisdom badly needs to be reassessed.

We believe we have also demonstrated the possibility and utility of historical trend analysis of national dependency. The dependency literature has devoted considerable attention to specifying *types* of dependency; it has given very little attention to describing *degrees*

113

of dependency among countries or within the same country over time. The kind of analysis used in this essay can illuminate, even if not answer definitively, questions about the degree of national dependency over time. By taking the degree of national dependency as an open and "researchable" question, this approach avoids both the liberal fallacy that sees Latin American countries as totally autonomous nations and the radical fallacy that sees them as totally helpless dependencies. One can treat these questions of national autonomy-dependency as continuous rather than dichotomous, and as weaves of thread going different directions at different times and rates on different levels. Thus this kind of analysis provides a more subtle, differentiated, historically informed approach than is presently the norm in writings about dependency.

This analysis has extended only from 1964 to 1975. One could easily deepen the historical perspective and conduct the same general type of analysis back to 1946, or to 1930, or indeed to the middle of the nineteenth century. The prevailing perspective in the dependency literature is that, on the whole, international penetration and constraints have intensified during the century and a half since formal independence. How well would this hypothesis stand up under serious testing? It would be interesting and worthwhile to find out, or at least to try.[37]

Our conclusions about trends in Brazilian dependency bear certain similarities to a few other recent studies about Latin America. For example, in Chile the secular trend since the beginning of World War II has been to reduce dependence on foreign investment in the copper industry. In his important study Moran shows how expanding economic resources, increasing technical and managerial competence in the copper industry, and the disintegration of a pro-American political coalition, all indexed a decline in Chilean national dependence from 1940 to the present.[38] Tugwell comes to similar conclusions about Venezuela and the oil industry.[39] Taken together these

---

[37] An excellent source for such an analysis would be Richard Graham, *Britain and the Onset of Modernization in Brazil, 1850-1914* (Cambridge: Cambridge University Press, 1968). Graham gives a rich, balanced account of the ways British influences did and did not help "modernization" in Brazil. During the nineteenth century the British controlled a number of important economic activities—export firms, the shipping industry, banking, railroads—which today are controlled by Brazilians. The argument that Brazil's dependency has increased since 1850 has to confront these facts.

[38] Theodore H. Moran, *Multinational Corporations and the Politics of Dependence: Copper in Chile* (Princeton: Princeton University Press, 1974).

[39] Franklin Tugwell, *The Politics of Oil in Venezuela* (Stanford, California: Stanford University Press, 1975).

and other studies[40] suggest that people writing about dependency have attended so much to national constraints (which of course exist and are very important) that they have neglected trends reducing those constraints.

---

[40] For a critique by a British Marxist of his fellow Marxists for underestimating the growth of national power in the Third World, see Bill Warren, "Imperialism and Capitalist Industrialization," *New Left Review*, no. 81 (September-October, 1973), pp. 3-44. Warren's study is amply documented. A thoughtful review-essay on recent studies is Richard S. Weinert, "Multinationals in Latin America," *Journal of Interamerican Studies and World Affairs*, vol. 18, no. 2 (May 1976), pp. 253-260.

CONTRIBUTORS

WERNER BAER is professor of economics at the University of Illinois at Urbana-Champaign. He has taught at Harvard, Yale, and Vanderbilt universities as well as at the University of São Paulo and the Getulio Vargas Foundation in Brazil. Dr. Baer has served as a program advisor in economics to the Ford Foundation in Brazil since 1967. He is the author of *Industrialization and Economic Development in Brazil* (1965), *Inflation and Growth in Latin America* (edited with I. Kerstenetzky 1970), and *The Development of the Brazilian Steel Industry* (1969).

WILLIAM R. CLINE is a senior fellow in the Foreign Policy Studies Program at the Brookings Institution. He is the author of *International Monetary Reform and the Developing Countries* (1967), *Potential Effects of Income Redistribution on Economic Growth: Latin American Cases* (1972), and *Economic Consequences of Land Reform in Brazil* (1970). Dr. Cline has taught at Princeton University and has served as a Ford Foundation visiting professor at the Brazilian Planning Ministry in Rio de Janeiro.

ROBERT A. PACKENHAM is an associate professor of political science and a faculty associate of the Institute of Political Studies at Stanford University. Dr. Packenham was a fellow at the Woodrow Wilson International Center for Scholars in Washington, D.C., in 1973–1974. He is the author of *Liberal America and the Third World: Political Development Ideas in Foreign Aid and Social Science* (1973) and articles on political development.

THOMAS E. SKIDMORE is professor of history at the University of Wisconsin. He was a Guggenheim fellow in 1974–1975 and a fellow at the Woodrow Wilson International Center for Scholars in Washington, D.C. in 1971–1972. He is the author of *Politics in Brazil, 1930–1964: An Experiment in Democracy* (1969), and *Black into White: Race and Nationality in Brazilian Thought* (1974). Dr. Skidmore served as president of the Latin American Studies Association in 1972.